ACKNOWLEDGEMENTS

I would like to express my sincere thanks to the people with whom I've worked to create this book, for the content ideas and the support I needed to complete it.

My husband for all his help, support and understanding. What I have achieved would not have been possible without him and I will always be sincerely grateful.

My family and friends who have always inspired and encouraged me to aim to be the best that I can in all that I do.

My clients: without them my journey would not have been as fulfilling as it has been and I would not have gained the experience and knowledge necessary to write this book.

My Associate VA, who without her help and support I would not be able to manage as many clients as efficiently and effectively as I do and would not be able to take a holiday!

INTRODUCTION

How many times have you thought about starting your own business as a virtual assistant, being your own boss, having a work/life balance and choosing what _you_ would like to do - but have never managed to get beyond the 'thinking' point?

How often have you looked at your current virtual assistant business and wished you could do more to develop it, but didn't know where to begin?

Don't worry. I know exactly what this feels like, because I have been there myself.

You will find no fluff, gimmicks or false promises here. Just lots of useful, practical and important information. Running a successful business takes a lot of hard work and commitment, but never let that put you off. You _can_ do it, just in the same way as I and many others have.

What I am sharing with you in this book is something that is simply not available on the internet: **_experience_**! I will be revealing my successes and failures: yes, we all fail at something in our lifetime, but learning from those mistakes can help us to grow and develop as individuals. You should never be afraid of making mistakes, just learn from them! I'll help you to avoid the pitfalls I encountered on the way to becoming a successful and professional virtual assistant and self-employed business owner.

This book will give you a kick up the **V.A.S.S (Virtual Assistant Support Services)** ladder by giving you a **_massive_** head start in setting up and developing a virtual assistant business.

It's intended as an in-depth guide: something you can read in your own time and refer back to when you feel the need. This book is not a 'get rich quick' solution or a 'set up fast' programme, it is more of a 'get set up *properly*' guide. I have poured as much information and as many tips, relevant links and practical tasks into this book as I possibly can, alongside my experience of what works and what doesn't.

If you are exploring the idea of setting up your own virtual assistant business from home, then this book has been written for you. Likewise, if you are looking to develop and improve your virtual assistant business, if you are someone looking to see if working from home is an option for you, or if you are just looking for some help and support with self-development, then this book has been written for you too.

So stop just dreaming about owning, running or developing your own business – make it actually happen! All you have to do now is make the best possible start by reading this book and taking action! Good luck!

Contents

PART 1 – GETTING STARTED

What is a Virtual Assistant?

A virtual assistant (typically abbreviated to VA) is a self-employed professional who provides administrative, technical or creative (social) assistance to clients either remotely from a home office, at the premises of a client or from rented office space.

There are many reasons why a business would choose to hire a virtual assistant, they are independent contractors (rather than employees), meaning that clients are not responsible for any employee related taxes, insurance, holiday or sick pay. Clients also avoid the logistical problem of having to provide extra office space, equipment or supplies. Essentially, clients pay for 100% productivity and can work alongside virtual assistants to ensure they get the exact, tailored support, they need.

Virtual assistants tend to come from a variety of business backgrounds, but most of them have several years' experience gained whilst working within the non-virtual business world.

Typically, 5 years or more of administrative or business support experience is expected of VAs holding positions such as Executive Assistant.

Why should you become a Virtual Assistant?

Because you are great at what you do! Let's face it, if you weren't, you wouldn't have been working in the world of admin or business support for as long as you have!

The world needs you! With an ever-changing world of business and advancements in technology, more and more business owners are turning to innovative and new ways of working.

You have a lot to offer! It's time to share your skills, knowledge and experience with those who need them.

Ambition! This is your opportunity to fulfil that strong desire for achievement.

Job satisfaction! You'll reap the rewards of all your hard work and effort.

Variety! *You* are in control of the type of work you get to do.

Choose who you work with! Not only do you get to choose the work you'd like to do, you also get to choose who you work with! *You* have the power to say 'no'.

Sense of achievement and self-respect! Everything you achieve is down to *your* hard work and effort.

Income! Get paid for doing a job that you love doing!

Work/life balance! Work when you want to and set the ground rules for the hours and days of the week you'd like to work.

Be your own boss! It's a wonderful feeling and one you will adapt to much more quickly than you think.

Your legacy! Your business can give you something to leave to a loved one if you build it into a company with employees.

The only regret I've had about becoming a virtual assistant is that I didn't do it sooner. I always had an excuse: the time wasn't right, I didn't have the money, did I have the knowledge and skills I needed, what if the client asked me to do something that I couldn't do? All of these 'fears' kept me from doing the one thing I really wanted to do. But once I got my business off the ground, I never looked back and I love what I do today just as much as I did when I first started.

So think about what is stopping you. What are your fears? Are they 'actual' or something that is just in your mind? What proof and evidence do you have that your fears are a reality? You know, most of the things we worry about never actually happen!

There's no right or wrong time to set up a business. When I started my business the country was coming out of recession, but I know a few virtual assistants who started in that recession and actually had *more* work during it. Think about it: in times of recession, businesses are looking for cost-effective ways to manage their business support needs. Virtual assistants offer the perfect solution in these circumstances.

You can even start your business whilst working full time in another role. It's hard work as you'll have to work evenings and weekends but it will.....

- Help you decide if running your own business is for you
- Give you time to build up your client base
- Offer you an opportunity to build your brand and reputation within the business marketplace
- Provide you with time to set up your business in general – open social media accounts, create your website etc
- Assess if you have everything you need
- Look into business insurance cover and other necessities

When you feel the time is right, you can start to work on your business in a full-time capacity. Only you can decide when that time is.

PRACTICAL TASK #1

First, I want you to create a document with three columns. The first column should be headed '**Why I want to be a VA**', the second '**What I want to achieve as a VA**' and the third '**Why I feel being a VA might not be for me**'. Look at the reasons for and against but don't worry if some cross over.

This exercise will help you to ultimately make a decision on whether or not being a virtual assistant is the right choice for you.

How long does it take to become a Virtual Assistant?

First let's define what is meant by 'become' a virtual assistant. This means the length of time it takes you to set up your business, this does not include growing and developing your business, as this takes many months and years to do.

- Setting up your business should take no more than one month.

- Growing and developing your brand, name and reputation within the marketplace takes many months and years to achieve. However, that doesn't mean it takes you months and years to find clients, it just means that you and your business will always be developing and changing and these changes take time. As you take on clients, you will begin to see the enhancements in your personal development as well as the growth of your business.

If you commit both time and effort to setting up and growing your business, you will be the business owner you have always dreamed of:

- Being your own boss
- Deciding who you would like to work with and for
- Be in control of the services you would like to offer
- Set the hours and days you want to work
- Feeling valued and appreciated
- Feeling a sense of achievement at the end of a working day

So…how can you achieve all of this? Simply by following this book and being prepared to work for it! It's a fact that if you don't let people know what you do, that you exist and how you can help them, you will never make an income or grow your business.

Your first steps to becoming a self-employed business owner start right here!

FAQs

When I first started my business I had so many questions, but not all of the answers I was looking for. I have set out below the questions I asked myself and, having been an executive virtual assistant for several years, I have the answers and I am now sharing these with you! I hope they help in making the decisions that are right for *you* and *your* business. Most start-ups ask the same questions and so you are not alone!

Q.1 Will I be able to make enough money to live on and pay the bills?

If you complete your business plan and carefully complete your cashflow sheet, this will give you a very good idea of what money you need to earn.

Q.2 Would I be able to keep my employed job for a while until I get my business off the ground?

Definitely, but think of this as a business and not a job. You can outsource work to other associates that you are unable to do yourself and make an income from that whilst you are setting up.

Q.3 Can being a Virtual Assistant be lonely?

As a virtual assistant you are never alone, you are part of a community. You will have contact with clients and associates. You will also be attending networking and other events to help build your business and your business contacts and don't forget you have social media too.

Q.4   Who would cover me for holidays or if I get ill?

Your associates will cover your holidays or period of illness if needed. You will need to let them know what they need to do and ensure they have thorough notes – contact names, phone numbers etc.

Q.5   What if I got so much work and could not cover it all by myself and meet the deadlines?

Other associates are the answer to this question. Many virtual assistants work with associates for this very purpose. If you were minded, you could also employ other people to work for you and have your own team.

Q.6   What if a client asked for a service I did not provide?

This is where building your support network comes into effect. Whether it is web development, call handling, there are people who can help and you can also earn money from referral fees.

Q.7   What if a client asked me to do something I can't do?

Virtual assistants who just start out always worry about this – I did myself! But there is no need. Simply ask your client to train you if it is one of their systems, I have never had a client who has objected or found this to be unexpected. You can also ask associates for help, you also have the internet and virtual assistant Facebook forums/support groups. You will find the virtual assistant community very supportive and eager to help.

Q.8   What if I do not get any clients?

You will.   It is just a matter of time.

Q.9   How long would it take to get my first client?

This depends on how much time and effort you put into finding one, but once you have found your first client, others will follow.

Q.10   What if I did not like being a business owner as much as I thought I would?

I personally don't know of any virtual assistants who have regretted starting their own business or want to go back to being employed.   However, if you do find yourself in this situation you can always go back to being employed.   One of the things you have to bear in mind is you will need to find another virtual assistant who can take over the management of your existing client(s), but this should not be too difficult as you can ask on VA forums on Facebook.

Q.11   How do I ensure that my skills are kept up to date?

The simplest answer is training, this may be by attending courses or by 'learning on the job' (self-teaching).   You should always ask clients to give you training on their specific systems, if needed.

Q.12   What resources are available to me to help me grow and develop my skills and knowledge of being a virtual assistant/freelance PA?

First, you have this book, I wrote this based on the many questions I am often asked by fellow virtual assistants at networking events, over the phone, via social media and emails and through my own experience. This book will give you loads of information and the tools you need to set-up and grow your own business. You will find many links to some of my favourite programmes/apps/software towards the back of this book.

Q.13 If there are many other virtual assistants in business, will I get enough work?

Some virtual assistants will have a specific niche. You will find that no two virtual assistants are exactly alike, they all offer different services and in different ways. There is room for everyone and if you work hard on your business, you will get work!

Q.14 How can I ensure success?

By working hard on your business and setting up properly you will significantly increase your chances of success.

Q.15 Is there demand for virtual assistants?

More and more business owners are looking for innovative ways of working. There are more businesses than ever before looking for affordable and flexible admin and business support, without the red tape and overheads. Virtual assistants are filling that need and with the advancements of technology it is becoming more commonplace for businesses to outsource their admin and business support services on a global scale.

Q16 What insurances do I need?

Primarily Professional Indemnity (this covers omissions and errors) and Public Liability (this covers you for working at the premises of your client or if you have people who will be visiting your office).

Q17 Can I work with flexible hours

You can work the days and hours you like, but you will need to ensure that you get your client's work completed on time, as agreed with them.

Q18 Can I just work as an associate to other virtual assistants?

Yes, you can, however, you will then be reliant on them to provide work for you and this may not be enough to give you the income you need. It also means you are not in control of your own business.

Q19 How do you get work to and from clients?

There are many ways to do this – it can be via email, by WeTransfer, USB stick, cloud based systems that your client may have that you can log into. Some clients drop work off in person if you are local to them.

Your Business Plan – what it should look like

When you start a business, one of the first things you should do is prepare a business plan. You will need to document why you are setting up a business in the first place, identify who your clients are, who is needed to run and manage the business, what finances you will need to set up and have a survival plan in place, find out if you may need to take out a loan and many other factors that come with running your own business.

If you need to take out a bank loan to start your business, the bank will want to see your business plan to evaluate its viability before agreeing the loan. The same also applies to any grants you may apply for, you will need to demonstrate that your plan has a good chance of success.

There is no law that says you have to have a business plan in place, but the ones that do generally go onto develop a successful business.

Let's now look at what your business plan should look like and include:

1. **Title Page** (front sheet)

    This should include your business name, logo (if you have one), address, phone numbers, web address, email address, your own name and revision date/number of the latest revision (the revision date/number is important, this is because your business will change as it grows and develops) and you should update your business plan as you progress to help keep you on track. You should change the revision date/number each time – e.g. 12 June 2018: Rev 1, the next time you amend it you should change this to, e.g. 16 October 2018: Rev 2 and so on.

2. **The Executive Summary**

    - This should be no more than 1-2 pages in length
    - This is the very last part of the plan to be written
    - It is a summary of what, where when, who and how – your vision for the business
    - It outlines the headline costs, the environment needed and likely returns

3. **Table of Contents**

Each section and page should be numbered and it should not, preferably, go beyond one page.

Section 1 – Objectives

The main aims and objectives of the business and your own personal aims and you may also like to include a mission statement (a mission statement is a short description of a company's function, its reason for being, the reason for its existence, its business goals and philosophies).

- What do you personally want to achieve and why?

- What do you want out of this achievement for yourself? Success, status, kudos, money, a better work/life balance? Where do other people fit in? Is this a shared ambition or are you doing this alone?

- What is your idea 'exactly' – what services are you going to provide? Where has your idea come from – what made you choose to become a virtual assistant? What gave you the idea – were you looking for job stability? A better work/life balance? Other?

- Is your idea your own or is it shared with someone?

- Have you told anyone else about your idea? Who have you told and what have you told them?

- What do you really want from a business – to be your own boss, money, shared achievement?

- What do you want for your business – retirement plan, steady or rapid growth?

- Not every goal and ambition will be reached at the same time, but what is your estimate for how long it will take you to achieve the bulk of your ambitions?

Section 2 – Abilities

- State the personal strengths and weaknesses of you and all key principals?

- Give brief details of experience, motivation and what you bring to the business, do not write your whole C.V., as you can append this at the back of your business plan. Why are you the right person to run this business?

- Who are the key personnel and what training (if any) may be required?

As you get busier with clients, you may need an associate virtual assistant, someone who can help you with a busy workload or cover for you in the event of illness or holidays. This should be covered in this section – you do not need to enter a specific name just 'Associate Virtual Assistant' will suffice for now.

Section 3 – Business Description

Give a summary of the service you will be offering. Who is it for? Who will buy it? Where will they come from? What will be your business process (how are you going to deliver your service)?

Section 4 – Market Research

How are you going to undertake this research – describe the methods you are going to employ?

- Identify your client base. Who are they? Where will they come from?

- Who are likely to be your competitors? Make an analysis of them.

- Consumer reaction – how are perceived clients going to react to your service or product?

- What research are you going to do to verify there is a demand for your service or product?

- How will you know if there is a want or need in the marketplace?

- Who are your competitors and where are they?

- What services or products do they supply?

- What do they do now that makes you identify them as competitors?

Section 5 – The Marketing Plan

- Identify the benefits and USP (Unique Selling Point) or 'niche' of your services or product? If you don't have one, don't worry, you may discover this later and, if you can't, then being a 'generalist' may be an option for you.

- What *are* the benefits?

- Where will you/your services be based? Where will you connect with your clients? What facilities will be required etc?

- What is your clear and reasoned pricing policy?

- What are your initial plans for promotion of your services or products?

- How are you going to reach your market – pricing, advertising, social media campaigns, business and social networking?

- Carry out a SWOT (Strengths, Weaknesses, Opportunities and Threats) and PESTEL (Political, Economy, Social, Technology, Environmental, Legal) analysis. This only needs to be a short list.

- Projected sales targets must be realistic to achieve and justified.

- Where do you think the business opportunity is?

- Who do you perceive your clients to be? What do you think are their wants or needs that make them your ideal clients?

- What is happening now? What do your perceived clients do now to satisfy their wants or needs? Is there already an existing product or service being supplied into the marketplace for them? What's wrong with it as far as your client is concerned?

Section 6 – The Organisational Plan – Logistics

- Give a description of the business and how it will operate – what is the business model to be employed?

- What will be the legal structure of the business? Sole trader, partnership, limited company?

- What type of premises, equipment, insurances etc will be required?

Section 7 – The Financial Plan

What are the detailed assumptions regarding income (sales forecast) ongoing expenditure and cost of sales/overhead costs, initial 'capital costs' and other start – up costs?

- Projected Profit and Loss Account for the first three years (what do you think you will earn or lose in the first three years?)

- Break even calculations

- Cash flow forecast for the first three years (each year on a separate sheet)

- Sensitivity analysis, e,g. how will you balance the books if sales do not reach 100% of forecast (pessimistic view)? Or what is the impact if sales reach 125% of forecast (optimistic view)? – pessimistic -v- optimistic, be realistic

- What funding will be required to start up – what will be your own financial contribution versus any loans, overdrafts, grants?

- What is your personal survival budget – what is your fall-back position (these details go into the appendices at the back of your business plan).

Section 8 – Appendices

These are the supporting documents to append at the back of your business plan and may include:-

- Your C.V.

- Market research data and competitor analysis papers

- Terms and conditions of supply of services (Client Contract)

- Privacy Policy – for your website - to demonstrate compliance with GDPR (more on this later)

- Associate Agreement (this is an agreement that one virtual assistant will have with another virtual assistant.

Don't worry about filling in your business plan just yet. As you work your way through this book it will help you to find many of the answers you will need.

Your Business Continuity/Disaster Recovery Plan

What would happen if you should ever have to go into hospital for an operation and unable to work for a while. What if you had a fire (heaven forbid!) – something that would make it extremely difficult to carry on working for your clients until you have resolved the problem? This is where your Business Continuity Plan comes into effect. This document is the creation of a strategy that recognises threats and risks to a business in the event of a disaster – or in simplistic terms – what are you going to do if a disaster should strike? This is a way of documenting your plan of action.

What should a business continuity plan contain?

No matter what type of business you are, there are seven key elements that every business continuity (or disaster recovery plan if you prefer) should contain:

1.   Initial Response

When something happens that disrupts day to day business operations it is important that everyone understands what they should do, if anything, immediately.

Whoever notices that something is wrong, they should know what to do, like dialling 999, or setting off the fire alarm.

Decision makers will need to be identified so that they can be notified in the event of an emergency or incident, along with their contact details and these should be added to any business continuity plan document. It is important for people to know 'who is in charge'

2.　　Steadying the Ship

Regardless of cause, every disruption needs to be dealt with in the same way. The first objective is to stop the situation from getting worse. You need to understand (1) what happened (2) how it happened (3) the potential impact if it is left unchecked. There won't be time to make a full-blown analysis and wait for further information.

3.　　Assessment

Once an assessment has been made, you will then know what system need to be restored. Linking your business continuity plan to your assets/services that it is designed to recover (you will need to list your assets in your business continuity document, e.g. PC/Printer) this will enable the decision maker to decide what action plan needs to be implemented to get the systems up and running again. A decision also needs to be made as to who is responsible for the plan, what will they do, where will they do it and with who?

4.　　Communication

In the event of an incident, who needs to be informed? List your clients and your suppliers with their contact details, relevant personnel – who is going to call them? Do you have an associate virtual assistant that needs to be informed of what has happened?

5.　　Response

Following the Initial Response and completion of the initial Assessment, the decision maker may declare a 'disaster' and cite their Business Continuity Plan. The scope of the planned response should include:

- What happened?

- What was the impact?

- Do you have what you need to deliver the planned response to an incident, e.g people, technology, supplies?

- What are you going to do to recover the situation?

6.   Extended Response

Depending on what happened, it could take days, weeks or months for a normal return to work to happen.

What procedures are you going to put in place to ensure your client's work is dealt with as quickly and smoothly as possible?

Be prepared for a lengthy recovery.

What resources would you need to maintain a lengthy recovery? What resources/people would you need (IT technician, associate virtual assistant, supplies, equipment?) Will you need alternative temporary accommodation and where might this be (perhaps a family member or a friend's house)

7.   Back to Normal

When the disruption ends, there will be questions that need to be answered:

- How will your backlog of work be reduced?

- How will work be sorted into post event catch up and new 'normal' work?

- Who is going to deal with insurance claims and collate the information needs to make that claim?

I hope the above gives you food for thought, you do not need to have a massive document – you just need to say who is going to do what, where and when should anything happen. This is why having a Business Continuity Plan is a good idea – it helps you to prepare for the unexpected!

What do I need to set up a business from home?

To work from home, you should only buy relevant equipment and office supplies when you need them. In some cases your client may want you to use their own equipment and supplies, so in that case there is no need to 'stock up' unnecessarily. In fact, it's fairly likely that you already have all the basics you need.

- **A business plan:** Your business plan will change as your business grows, but it will act as a good guide in the early stages and help keep you on track. It will also act as a reminder as to why you set up your own business in the first place.

- **A good quality printer:** Preferably an all-in-one device, but start with the printer you may already own as that will be sufficient to begin with.

- **A PC/laptop that is used *solely* by you:** You will be using and storing your client's confidential information and this *must not* be compromised in any way.

- **An office suite of software:** (such as Excel, PowerPoint, Word, Outlook etc) I was fortunate that I started with the full Microsoft Office suite on my PC, but not everyone has access to this when they first start out. If you want 'cloud' (internet) storage space and access to all the familiar Word, Excel, PowerPoint, Outlook packages etc, you may want to take a look at the online 365 packages offered by Microsoft at very affordable prices. They have three plans and I personally use the Office 365 Business Premium package, which is loaded onto my desktop PC and laptop to give me a full mobile service. If this is of interest to you, you may like to take a look at the different packages on offer:

https://products.office.com/en-gb/business/compare-office-365-for-business-plans

- **A good, reliable internet connection**: Make sure it comes with a decent download speed too.

- **A phone**: Again, start with what you currently own. There are a number of further options available to you and we will look at these a little later.

- **A dedicated work area**: Ideally somewhere in which you can work in peace and quiet. If you have children and/or dogs it is not a good idea to have them running around and making a lot of noise in the background. You need to be able to focus clearly on your client and their needs, it's best to close the office door during working hours.

- **An open mind and an eagerness to learn:** You'll be learning more than you imagined was possible, but don't fear this. Embrace this new world of technology we live in and the new opportunities that go with it.

- **A business email address and domain name**: We'll examine these a little later.

- **An idea of the type of services you would like to offer**: You need to be clear about who your target market is. I found that trying to be everything to everybody didn't work, but I eventually decided on what route I wanted to take. When I followed that, I then discovered I had much greater client focus. *You cannot be everything to everybody*, so consider what you offer carefully. Make a list of services you can provide and assess which types of business would benefit from them.

- **Days and hours of work**: Decide how many days and how many hours you intend to work.

- **Positive support:** You'll need help and support from people around you, so try to stay clear of people who are constantly giving 'negative vibes'. These will be of no help or value to you. Constructive criticism: yes. Negativity: no

PRACTICAL TASK #2

You can upgrade or buy any equipment as you build your business, as you'll gain a better understanding of what you actually need. I remember buying some items and not using them for ages. It was wasted money, so only buy supplies as and when you need them.

For your next task, make a list of the necessary items that you already own. You should also list what you think you may need. This equipment check list, although not definitive, will act as a guide to help you start your business. Look at the items you are missing and use the internet to find how much each purchase costs, and add these details to your business plan.

I have set out below some suggested 'immediate' and 'as soon as possible' items to start your business that will help you to plan your financial outlay.

Immediate

- PC or Laptop
- Broadband
- Basic Stationery items (pens, pencils, sharpener, ruler, stapler)
- Notepad
- Telephone – landline and/or mobile (you can start with just a mobile and add the landline later)
- Business cards
- Insurance
- Email address (preferably business)
- Mini business plan
- Software package (e.g Microsoft Office 365)
- Register with ICO for GDPR (more on this later)
- Access to a diary (e.g. Google Calendar)
- Printer

As soon as possible/for you to think about

- Website, hosting and professional email address (if you used a Gmail (or similar) account to start with)
- Accounts spreadsheet
- Car-mounted advertisement
- Hard drive/external backup (important for GDPR compliance – covered later in this book)
- Client Contract
- Associate Agreement
- Website Privacy Policy

When you first start your business you want people to take you seriously and as a professional and it is important that you get your paperwork in order to ensure you get off on the right foot. I have listed below some of the templates I use on a day to day basis. These were templates I created and developed as my business grew and I still use them to this day. Having good templates will help you to work more efficiently, effectively and give that all important professional image when communicating with your clients.

Templates

Templates are a really good way of keeping your paperwork in order, organised and constructive. Over the years I have created my own templates that I use on a day to day basis. They are very easy to use, I do not need to pay any subscription fees for them and I can update them whenever I wish. Some of my favourite templates and ones I use very often are:

Potential Client Templates

- Client Information Pack (essential information your client will need)

- Client Assessment (what type of support does your client need?)

- Questions Prompt Sheet (going to meet a potential client – what questions are you going to ask them?)

- Client Proposal (this is what you would send to a potential client who enquires about your services)

- Feedback form (so you didn't get the work, but why?). Sending a very polite feedback form to potential clients who may have decided against working with you (don't worry, this happens to everyone at some point) may help you to improve your services. Some may prefer not to answer. Sometimes, it is because their circumstances have changed and are totally unrelated to what you offered, but it is nice to know that!.

New Client Templates

- Mileage log book (you will need to log your business miles for your bookkeeping purposes – business miles include going to collect stationery supplies etc for your client, attending business networking events, attending business shows with your client, driving to your client's premises etc, attending meetings with new or potential clients, these should all be logged as business miles – and remember to add the return journey!).

- Client Contract (an essential document which sets out very clearly your terms and conditions for the supply of services to your client and that your client should sign their agreement).

- Client and contact database (once you begin to take on clients and attend networking events, you will collect an array of business cards and I always add the contact details from these business cards to my contact database in the event I should need to contact someone I have met. As you begin to work with clients you will need to keep their log in and contact details somewhere safe and secure to accord with GDPR. You can add these to your database and add password protection to the document to keep it secure).

- Client check list (there are many things you need to remember to do when you take on new clients and so having a check list to hand for each client is a good way to keep track of what you have done and what you need to do).

- Client timesheet (I always like to provide my client with a timesheet, this keeps the working arrangement transparent and helps to keep a record of work undertaken and time spent on tasks).

- Client welcome letter (this is a letter you would send to a new client to welcome them on board).

Finance Templates

- Finance spreadsheet (this is where you record your outgoings and incomings – this helps you to keep track of your finances).

- First overdue payment letter (this is the first 'gentle nudge' letter you would send to a client who has not paid your invoice)

- Second overdue payment letter (this is a more 'direct gentle nudge' letter you would sent to a client who has not paid you following your first gentle nudge letter).

- Letter demanding payment (this is a letter you would send to a client - after sending the first and second overdue letters and doing all that is necessary to resolve any concerns the client may have with regard to the costs involved – this letter needs to be considered carefully and is a formal demand for payment of outstanding sums and needs to contain certain information).

- 'Letter Before Claim' (this is a letter you would send to a client who disputes the payment they owe you. This letter needs to be in accordance with the 'Practice Direction' – this is your starting point as a prospective claimant who has a claim for breach of contract. This letter must be sent to a client before commencing any legal proceedings, it must contain certain information in accordance with the Practice Direction and worded carefully. A court would want to see that you have done all that is necessary to try to recover the monies before issuing court proceedings. You can find more information about this here:

  https://www.citizensadvice.org.uk/law-and-courts/legal-system/taking-legal-action/small-claims/making-a-small-claim/

Training

Whether you need specific virtual assistant training really depends on your levels of experience and confidence. If you have many years' experience in an administrative/office management support role, this book may be all you need. There are specific virtual assistant training courses available and there are also many system specific training courses, e.g if your Word or Excel are a little rusty you may want to upskill. Whether you undertake training and in what format can only be decided by you, as only you know (1) how confident you feel (2) how many years' of experience you have under your belt and (3) what new skills you may need to learn.

Groupon and Udemy are good places to find training courses, but be selective, do not opt for the course which is the cheapest, go for the one that offers what you feel you need.
https://www.groupon.co.uk/
https://www.udemy.com/

Your phone number

Based on my own personal experience I would always recommend keeping your private and business phones separate once you are ready to begin taking on clients. This also matters when it comes to putting the cost of calls through your business accounts, as it is much easier and less time consuming to state on your accounts that all the calls on the bill are for business purposes.

It would be preferable to add a landline to your website (or do this as soon as possible if you need to start with a mobile number). It is all about perception: it really *does* matter and you need to ensure that everything you do is taken both seriously and professionally – and that includes the phones that you use in the running of your business.

As your client base grows, you may wish to consider hiring a call answering service to take calls for you or for your client.

Many virtual assistants collaborate with telephone call handling companies to take calls on behalf of their clients and they will offer a referral fee for doing so. You can ask on social media for recommendations, virtual assistant Facebook groups are always a good place to start, you will find many virtual assistants will be happy to recommend a call handling company to you.

There are companies who offer a virtual receptionist service one of the more popular providers for this is E-receptionist and you can find out more here:
https://www.ereceptionist.co.uk

Another option is a VOIP (Voice Over Internet Protocol) system. Many virtual assistants take advantage of these as they are easy to use. Some of the more popular VOIP system providers are:

https://www.ringcentral.co.uk
https://www.voipfone.co.uk/
https://business.bt.com/products/business-phone-systems/voip

There are many others available. Again, you can ask on virtual assistant forums on Facebook for recommendations.

You can also get 'virtual landline' numbers. When people call your virtual landline number, it goes straight to your mobile, but people think they are calling a landline. Ask your mobile provider if they offer this type of service and what their costs are. I have mine via Vodafone:
http://www.vodafone.co.uk/business/solutions/integrated-solutions/one-net-anywhere/index.htm

Telephone Handling Guide

We have all taken telephone calls, whether it be family, friends or a works phone, but when you are running your own business a little more is expected of you. I have set out below a basic guide which will help you get started and prepare.

Incoming phone calls can take up a lot of time and seriously dent your productivity by taking you away from other tasks. There are ways of handling incoming phone calls to cut down on the amount of time you use speaking on the phone. These top tips will help you to work smarter on your phone.

1. **Answer the phone with a proper business greeting**

    First impressions are the ones that get remembered and so always answer your phone with a proper business greeting. For example, when answering the phone say something along the lines of – 'Good morning/afternoon, [state your business name], [state your name] speaking. How may I help?' This not only lets the caller know they've reached the right business, but it also puts the onus on the caller to answer the question, saving time on exploratory questions such as, "Is this [your business name]?" and general 'chit chat'.

2. **Keep phone calls on track**

    If you're speaking to someone on the phone who seems to want to stray from the point, say something such as, "So what I hear you saying is..." or "So the main points are..." or "Is XXXXX a fair summary of what you are saying?" This helps keep the call on track.

3. **Try to form a habit of closing each incoming phone call with a summary of what you have agreed with the caller**

    In most cases this will only take a short time but it can save you a lot of time by avoiding mistakes and having to re-check. For example, if you have agreed to meet a client, you might say, 'Good. I'll meet with you at [location] on [date] at [time] and we'll discuss your requirements."

4. **Keep a message pad and something to write with handy, so you can take down any necessary details**

    This is good practice for any business. It keeps you focused on the call and it will also help later if you need to review the details of a particular phone conversation. For example, always take down the name of the caller, their contact number, the date and time they called, a brief summary of the conversation and a convenient time that you can call them back if this is what has been agreed. Remember to diarise any follow up work you need to do!

5. **If you're running a home-based business, get a separate business phone and/or line as soon as you can**

    You may need to have a second 'business only' phone with its own 'business only' answering machine and/or voice mail. Not only is this more professional but it will save you time in wading through numerous messages to find out which are personal and which are business related.

6. **Service with a Smile!**

    However you answer your phone, always do it with a smile – it really does help! When dealing with difficult calls or you are taking lots of calls in quick succession and it's interrupting your schedule and making you feel frustrated, just remember to smile and it *really will* help. It is important not to allow your frustrations to filter through to the caller.

7. **Sorry, I didn't quite catch that!**

If someone is calling from a mobile, remember to ensure there is a good connection, if the caller is in an area with limited signal, they may not be able to hear your first words, or they may not be able to hear you due to noise in the background. Let the caller know if you are having difficulty with the connection and apologise if you have to ask them to repeat information. This will save you and the caller time and help avoid any misinterpretation or misunderstanding.

8. **Using modern technology to help you manage the time you're spending answering the phone**

A minimum requirement for any modern-day business is an answer machine/voicemail set up. Set these up with an appropriate business greeting and let them answer the phone for you when you are out of the office or need to have some time uninterrupted. Ensure you make time to answer any messages that have been left for you each day.

9. **Confidentiality**

Be mindful when taking calls, as the conversation you are holding with the caller may be sensitive in nature and the conversation should remain private. People often forget this when taking calls on trains, in restaurants and many other public places.

10. **People prefer to talk to a person rather than a machine!**

Having a voicemail pick-up can be problematical in that people may dislike leaving messages and won't bother to call back. If answering incoming calls is taking up too much of your time, consider engaging a call handling service to answer the phone for you and to filter your calls.

Telephone Tips Summary

It may be worth remembering that the telephone is supposed to be a business tool, not an invasive time waster that rules your working day. Handling your incoming calls according to these tips will help you manage your time, improve your productivity and put your phone back where it belongs - helping **you** run your business rather than **it** running you.

PRACTICAL TASK #3

Take a moment to research VOIP systems on the internet. See what options are available and how VOIP might work for you. Compare what they offer.

https://www.ringcentral.co.uk
https://www.voipfone.co.uk/
https://business.bt.com/products/business-phone-systems/voip

Working Virtually, On-Site or Both?

If you have reached the stage where you're asking yourself this question then that's great! You've taken your first steps to becoming a self-employed business owner!

One of the main things you need to decide is where you are going to work from. This is your business and you, primarily, make all the decisions on whether you wish to work exclusively from home or are prepared to work at the offices of your client. There are a couple of things to bear in mind when making this decision:

- If you are starting from scratch with no clients (as I did), then money may play a big part in how you work at the beginning, and who with. Having some money to pay the bills is better than having none at all. As you establish your name and reputation within the market place and build your client base, you can then be more selective with regards to the type of clients you would like to work with, the sort of work you would like to do and where you would, primarily, like to work from.

- Can the tasks you are going to offer to clients be done from home?

Working from home

There are a few things you need to consider when working from home – the main one being, are you allowed to do so?

- If you have a Tenancy Agreement or Letting Agent, are there any planning restrictions for use of the premises? Check your documentation to see if any restrictions exist for working from home and, if so, contact the landlord or letting agent and see if you can negotiate a relaxation of the terms. If something in your terms says 'no', it doesn't necessarily mean that it can't be changed. If you are unsure, then just ask your Landlord or Letting Agent for clarification.

- Do you have a mortgage? If so there may be restrictive covenants (clauses) that forbid you running a business from home. However, this may not apply to your type of business. It's a good idea to check your mortgage conditions and if you are in any doubt speak to your mortgage lender or your solicitor for confirmation.

- If you own a home with no mortgage, it doesn't necessarily mean that you're okay to run a business from home simply because you own it. There may be specific terms and conditions of use in your planning permission that forbid you from running a business, so check this point before proceeding and try to negotiate a change with the local authority or via your solicitor if needs be.

- Do you have enough garden space to build a suitable office building? I know a few virtual assistants who've had wooden buildings erected in the garden and choose to work from those. Again, you'll need to do a thorough check of your planning restrictions and you should think about the security implications too. You may need to apply for planning permission.

- You will need to set some ground rules and *stick to them*. You will find that family and friends pop in for a coffee during working hours, simply because they know you are at home! They may ask you to accept parcel deliveries on their behalf because they know you are likely to be in to answer the door to the postman. You need them to take you and your business seriously and understand the boundaries.

- You may also get family and friends who ask you to help them out from time to time, which is fine, but remember, you are now a business and your family and friends are now your clients. It is okay to have 'mates rates' and I will cover this a little later.

- Do you have dedicated work space where you can close the door?

- Is the space you have big enough for you and the equipment you will need?

- Are your internet connection and download speeds sufficient for you to run a professional business support operation?

- Do you want to use your home address for contact purposes? If not then one option you might like to consider is a virtual office. This is an office address you can use for correspondence, while not having to actually work from it. This address can be used on your website and other communications. The Chamber of Commerce offer such offices at a reasonable monthly rate. You can ask them to contact you via email should you have any mail to pick up, or you can ask them to send your post to you, but this is a little more expensive. Using a virtual office also gives some security to your home address. Some people also use their accountants address. You could also use the PO Box of Royal Mail, but this is more expensive.
  http://www.britishchambers.org.uk/business/
  https://www.royalmail.com/personal/receiving-mail/po-box

- I managed to negotiate a change to my planning permission to allow me to work from home. It took a couple of phone calls and a letter to the local council, but after a couple of weeks it was all sorted. You just need to be polite, determined and persistent, but without being pushy.

Working from a client's premises

You'll find that you negotiate different working practices with each client, as they each will have different needs. For my own needs I created a separate client proposal for each while using the same standard template, enabling me to meet the needs and 'must haves' of each individual client. So when you're negotiating with potential clients, think about:

- Travel – how far are you prepared to travel? Remember to negotiate your time of travel and travel costs. While you are travelling you may not be earning money (depending on what mode of transport you are

using) and this needs to be taken into account. You can claim tax relief to a maximum of 45p per mile, without tax implications, which can be charged to the client if this is negotiated with them. Further details can be found here:
https://www.gov.uk/simpler-income-tax-simplified-expenses/vehicles-

- Do you want to state specific start and finish times and days of the week you work with clients?

- Is your client going to provide you with all the equipment and materials to carry out the work?

- How are you going to travel to your client's premises? Are you going to drive in your own car, take the train, tram or bus, or even simply walk? What is your 'Plan B' should your car break down, or if the public transport providers go on strike?

- Remember, clients are relying on *you* for help! It's vitally important that you build a reputation founded on reliability and trust. If you don't, then all that you have worked hard to build could be destroyed in no time at all.

Working from a rented office space

You may prefer to rent office space rather than work from home. There are now many start-up (sometimes called incubator) units available for rent, which help small businesses 'get off the ground' and, if you are considering this option, it may be worth you researching the internet for these types of unit close to where you are based. There are also business centres which offer rented office accommodation, but the rental cost of these are much higher. There are a few questions you will need to consider when making this decision:

- Do you have the necessary finances? What budget do you have? If you are considering using a local business centre, let the office space provider know that you are just starting out as a new business and see if you can negotiate a reduced rate – do they have introductory offers? If you are considering an incubator unit, you may find that these rates are set and are none negotiable.

- Could you possibly share an office with someone else? For example, do you know an IT professional or web designer who may be willing to rent you a space in their office? This could also give you an opportunity to share referrals with one another and build working relationships with them.

- Do you need or want a shared receptionist to take your calls and handle your incoming/outgoing mail?

- Can you have your own phone line and internet connection? What are the internet speeds? How will calls be charged?

- Is there an opportunity to gain work from tenants if you opt for renting an office in a business centre?

- Is the space you're interested in available immediately, or is there a waiting list?

- Is a meeting room available for your use if required? What's the cost and terms of use? Does it meet your needs?

- Does the office space come with office furniture? Would you have use of a desk, chair and storage space?

PRACTICAL TASK #4

Have a think about the options I've outlined above and write down the advantages and disadvantages for each. This will help you to decide which option is most suited to you and your business at this point in time.

Whichever option you decide to follow requires serious consideration, thought, planning and research. Remember, you can always change your mind at a later date if you feel you need to.

Researching your Competitors and your Target Market

By now, you have decided what work you would like to undertake and where you are going to operate your business from. You now need to look at the work of your competitors and establish your target market.

As technology has advanced greatly over the years and cloud computing has become more commonplace within the world of business, the virtual assistant industry (and indeed home working in general), is rapidly expanding on a global scale, resulting in competition in all industries. Don't be afraid of competition, it helps keep you on your toes! Competition is healthy. It's about you being better than your competitors, offering something different and offering something that people want. What need are you going to fill? How are you going to solve your client's problems?

To find out, start by carrying out a little research into other virtual assistants. You'll soon discover that no two virtual assistants are the same. Each has their own niche, ways of working, and a different range of services on offer to their clients. Start by researching which virtual assistants are offering similar services to you. Where are they based? Nationally? Locally?

Pay particular attention to the virtual assistants who are offering the same services as you. Look at their websites. What are they charging? How do they describe their services and their business? Take notes of what you like and what you don't like. What do you feel works? What doesn't? Please do not copy the content from other virtual assistant websites – make yours unique to you!

Go back to the list of services you made: does a particular type of client stand out? Medical professionals, third sector/charitable organisations, construction, authors, busy executives, start-ups, actors? Try to identify at least two that grab your attention. It may take you longer than you expect to reach one type of client and so it makes sense to have two or three to go at.

Now you need to find your clients, based on the sectors you've selected. Search the internet to find out where they hang out. Which networking events do they attend? Take a look on social media to find out if they are on Facebook, LinkedIn, Twitter, or Google+ etc. You might find the relevant social media links on their websites, but this is not guaranteed. For example, builders may be listed on Facebook, while busy executives may be on LinkedIn only.

Narrow down your research by focusing on your chosen method of working. If you prefer to totally work on site then search locally, but if you choose to work primarily from home, then search globally. Take your time with this as research into knowing and understanding your competitors and potential clients is fundamental to *your* success.

Check through the list of services you intend to offer to potential clients that you created earlier. Is there a strong enough client base for your type of services? Can you make enough money from the services you are offering? You may need to re-visit your list and either reduce or expand it.

Do you have a niche? Something that sets you apart from your potential competitors? If so, it will be much easier to market yourself. You may not have yet worked out what your niche is, but that doesn't mean you have nothing to offer. We all have something to offer, it is just a case of figuring out what it is. I do know some virtual assistants who discovered their niche whilst working with particular types of client – they like the type of work they do for them and then decide to focus on that particular market.

Exploring your niche – do you have one and do you need one?

McDonalds, Starbucks, KFC, Coca Cola and IKEA all did it and I am sure you recognise these names – all of them now worldwide business powerhouses. They created their own very successful business niche. McDonalds focused on fast food - can you remember interesting fast food before they came along? IKEA introduced affordable flat packed furniture that made having a stylish and modern home available to all. You get the picture.

Business today is more competitive than ever. For almost every type of business or product you'll find a competitor selling or offering something the same or at least very similar. If you can, you need to separate yourself from your competitors by offering something that no one else does or by targeting your business offering and marketing to attract potential clients.

By delivering a service that fills a need, your clients will wonder how they managed to cope without you. Is there a service you can offer that a competitor has failed to fulfil? Can you become a specialist in an area filled with 'generalists'?

Try not to be everything to everybody. It will help you to focus on the specific expertise you may have to offer in a particular area or field. Have you worked in a particular medical sector? Have you worked in a specific marketing sector? These specialist skills could set you apart from generalists and it's worth bearing in mind that you can charge more for your specialist knowledge and skills. Why? Because you understand the specialist words and phrases and you may know specific ways to help a client to get their message out with targeted and well-informed marketing content.

Finding a niche can often be a matter of putting a new spin on what you already do. How can you differentiate your business from that of your competitor? What do you have to offer? Make a list of what you can do and find out if there is a particular market that could benefit from those particular skills. Ask yourself this question: "How can I create the perception that the market simply can't live without my help?"

You need to decide who you want your clients to be. Choose your focus carefully. If you have problems with this, start by examining the needs of your clients and match your services to fill their needs. This way they are more likely to want to buy from you. Is there a market for your services? Is it a strong enough market to make your niche viable?

It's important to never rest on your laurels however. To help unlock exactly what your niche is, you could brainstorm your ideas with someone else. Is there someone you know who you could discuss this with, someone who understands the virtual assistant community? It can be amazing what other people can see that you may have missed. Once you've found your niche, you then need to keep things fresh. Do this exercise again. The market is always changing and it is important that you do not become 'stagnant'. You need to put yourself in a position to be able to meet the ever changing needs of businesses. Introduce new services and/or products, create your own networking group to raise your profile, give a presentation at an event. There are many things you can do to showcase your specialist skills.

The above said, if you don't have a niche, don't' worry about it, there are many generalist virtual assistants making a good living, they just charge a little less than those who have a specialist niche. There is room for both in the very busy business world we live in today.

Naming Your Business

Naming your business is something to consider very carefully. This will be a huge part of your brand and your future. This is who your client will be buying services from. It should not be taken lightly. Take your time with this and consider:

- Will people 'get it'? Will they understand what you are all about at a glance?

- Will you use your own name as your company name?

- Is there anyone else already using the name you'd like to use?

- Think about your client market: will your chosen name register with them easily and quickly?

- Think about the future: will your name grow with you? I started out as a Virtual PA but then later became a Business Centre instead as my business grew and the demands of clients became more and more varied and demanding.

- How are you planning to describe yourself? Are you going to be a virtual assistant, business consultant, freelancer or specialist? Believe it or not, there are a lot of business owners out there who are still unsure as to what a virtual assistant actually is and what they do!

When considering my business name I asked myself three questions:

(1) Who would clients actually be buying the services from?
(2) Who would clients be working with?
(3) Whose brand would I be building?

In each case, the answer was 'me'. I would be the business owner and the actual brand and so I opted to use my maiden name which was 'Wright'. My business became Wright Business Support Centre and my slogan grew from my business name too: "the Wright services, at the Wright time and at the Wright price – the Wright choice". On a more subtle level, this is where the 'tick' mark idea came from that has since been used in my business logo. Remember the days when you got a 'tick' at school for getting the right answer? Can you see how I built the idea? It just involved a little bit of 'thinking differently' before carefully choosing my business name and creating my logo. Have a careful think about what you could call your business, why and how you could connect this to your logo.

Building your Support Networks

Building strong support networks will be crucial to the growth and development of your business. It's really important to surround yourself with positivity, knowledge and experience. There will be times when you hit problems while running your business. I hit plenty of them when I first started out and I still do, and so do other businesses. Don't worry – that's just normal! Having support mechanisms and good people around you will help you through those difficulties in the same way that my contacts helped me. I am often asked questions by fellow virtual assistants who need help and advice and that's why I decided to write this book, in the hope it will answer a lot of those queries and prove to be of help to you.

So...how and where can you make contacts?

First, start at home with your family and friends. They'll be the first supportive ear and arm around your shoulder should you hit any problems. Remember, problems are par for the course in business, but you will get through them and the experience will make you all the more stronger for it.

Next, consider fellow virtual assistants. You might be surprised at how supportive and helpful other virtual assistants can be. It certainly took me by surprise. When I first started out I met my first fellow virtual assistant at a networking event (more on networking later). I was introduced to her by someone who thought we'd have things in common and a good potential for synergy. Well, I have to be honest and say that this is not the way I saw it! I simply thought 'Oh great, a local competitor, that's all I need!' How wrong I was. I am so glad I decided to speak to her as it was quite possibly the best thing I did in the early phase of growing my business. I quickly learned that my fellow virtual assistant was an 'opportunity', not a threat. There is room for all of us!

I discovered that other virtual assistants are a community all of their own. They collaborate and are happy to share. I saw other virtual assistants in a totally different light after meeting and speaking with my fellow virtual assistant, who is now my trusted and reliable associate. We now share clients, cover for each other, bounce ideas off one another and have become close friends as well as work colleagues and, to this very day, we still collaborate on many topics and projects. Working on your own can, at times, seem a lonely place, but it's good to know that another virtual assistant is just a phone call, email away or Facebook group away!

PRACTICAL TASK #5

Take a look at the following organisations and familiarise yourself with the help and support available to you outside of virtual assistant circles. Have a look through these websites and see what services and events they offer. Read their blog posts and see what people are chatting about: what kind of support are people looking for? Can you fulfil that need with your services?

The Federation of Small Businesses (FSB) - an organisation offering business support services and events.
http://www.fsb.org.uk/

The Princes Trust: a great organisation which can help you develop your business idea if you're aged 18-30, living in the UK, and unemployed or working fewer than 16 hours a week.
https://www.princes-trust.org.uk

British Chamber of Commerce: an organisation offering business support and events, along with a host of other member benefits.
http://www.britishchambers.org.uk/

The British Government have many free resources to help many small businesses within the UK.
https://www.gov.uk/business-support-helpline

Working with Associate Virtual Assistants

Okay, first things first. What exactly is an Associate Virtual Assistant? Well, put simply, it's a virtual assistant who you are able to sub-contract work to, should you find yourself very busy and need help or unable to complete a task set by your client because you don't personally have the relevant skill set to complete it.

Personally, I have found working with other virtual assistants to be a really beneficial experience. You can bounce ideas off them, they offer support, they can help lighten your workload at busy times and can help with tasks that you may not have experience in handling. They can also cover for you if you are unwell or away on holiday. We all need a holiday don't we! Don't forget: it's a two-way process and you can offer your associate the same service in return.

It's very important that you build a professional relationship with any associate you feel you would like to work with. You need to feel happy that they can take care of your clients in your absence and continue to provide them with the same level of service that you would deliver yourself. Think ahead: you may need to give your associate your log-in details along with other important pieces of confidential information and it is your name and reputation that is on the line, so choose an associate very carefully.

It is always best to have an Associate Agreement with fellow professionals. This document sets out what you have agreed with each other and what is expected from one another. It ensures that you and your associate both know where you stand.

You will find it common practice amongst associate virtual assistants to work for you at a lesser rate when you sub-contract work to them. This is because they do not have to find the work themselves, but you would ordinarily need to liaise with the client and invoice them directly, and so you need to ensure your costs are covered in the process. For example, if I was to charge a client, say, £25 per hour for a specific task and I sub-contracted this task to my associate, we may agree that he/she receives £18 per hour and I keep the other £7 per hour to cover my own costs. The cost to the client remains the same. The splitting of rates is something you would need to agree on an individual basis with your associate. Remember, that if your associate should sub-contract work to you, the same working process applies.

This brings me nicely to the subject of ethics! Personally, I would never approach the client of a fellow virtual assistant openly or knowingly. The virtual assistant community is very much one founded on collaboration and professionalism. Ask yourself this question: if a fellow virtual assistant should 'steal' your client, how would that make you feel? Not too good, I imagine.

When I sub-contract work to my associate I always bill the client personally. First, my associate sends me her invoice. I then add her costs to my costs. This is the invoice I then send to the client – I do not send the client the invoice of my associate virtual assistant – I only send the one I have prepared that contains both the costs of work I have undertaken and the costs of the work my associate has completed on my behalf. In this way, the client receives only one invoice.

In general I always liaise personally with the client, but if I am on holiday I will ask my associate to speak with them. Again, this is why it is vital that you build a trusting working relationship with your associate(s).

Meet up/speak to any potential associates and find out as much as you can about them. Ask about their standards and how they work. Start with simple tasks and consider asking your potential associate to bring along samples of work so that you can assess their suitability, ask them to carry out a task for you to see how they do.

Your associate virtual assistant will need to know about the work you will be setting them and the hours they will need to account for. It's helpful to create a document in advance, setting out all of the information an associate will need to complete tasks on your behalf.

As well as virtual assistant associates there are also other professional 'partner' associates you can work with such as web developers, telephone call handling companies and IT companies. As with associate virtual assistants, you should choose your partner associates very carefully and ensure they share the same high standards and levels of client focus as yourself. Partner associates can offer services which you may not (or do not want to) provide. Bear in mind that you can also ask your partner associates for a referral fee for any work that you put their way. For example, if you have a client who would like a call handling service, but you are unable or do not want to provide this yourself, you can pass this to your call handling associate in exchange for a referral fee. The same applies to IT or web/app/branding professionals and so on. This provides passive income for you. Make sure that you have a written agreement in place beforehand with your partner associates to ensure you get paid for any referrals you may make (this could be just an exchange of emails setting out the details).

Some virtual assistants do not use the referral fee mechanism and instead agree an exchange of services, for example, you could offer to work for free for an IT consultant and in return they may offer to look after your IT equipment for you, but this needs to be balanced and a set number of hours agreed or you could end up doing a lot of work for your consultant and they may offer much less in return.

Working with and Managing Clients

Each client you work with is equally important and will be unique in their own right. You will need to treat each client in the same way as the next however– they all deserve to receive the same level of service. They are relying on you to help run and manage *their* business, trusting you with *their* brand, name and reputation within the marketplace. They expect *you* to deliver on *your* promises.

I like to meet and speak with clients as much as possible, whether this is on the phone, at a meeting or online via Skype. It enables me to build up a good, professional relationship with them. How much contact you have may depend on the wishes of the client.

I allow one hour for client meetings, unless otherwise agreed with the client. Some clients may need longer if the purpose of the call is to discuss various work issues and schedules. Set times for your meetings; it helps to keep you productive.

The more of a professional relationship you build with your client, the easier it becomes to develop your workload with them. As clients become used to you and how you work, they may ask if they can pass other work on to you and, don't forget, you can suggest to your client that they consider passing you certain duties and/or responsibilities to free up more of their time, allowing them to concentrate on managing and developing their own business. After all, you are there to help ease their pressure points! Look at what they are doing and assess if there is anything more you can be doing to help them. What you are aiming for is repeat custom. It is much easier to run a business if you have a good idea of how much income you will generate each month. If you can tie your client into monthly retainers or contracts, this provides you with a steady, reliable monthly income. It is also better for your client as they know what they will be paying each month.

I provide my clients with a client contract that I ask them to sign prior to me undertaking any work for them. Having a signed agreement means each party knows what is expected and how the professional relationship is going to work. It sets some ground rules for the services I'm going to provide, covers how those services are going to be provided and how the client is expected to pay me for those services. It also covers working hours and my policies for out of hours working. This contract is essential as it binds the two parties together, everyone knows where they stand and it makes it far easier to deal with any dispute, it also keeps the contract UK based should you ever work with overseas clients.

Of course, we all hope to avoid disputes at all costs, but it is good to have a safety net, just in case.

Confidentiality Agreements

Some clients may ask you to sign a confidentiality agreement, or you may like to offer one to your client. This gives the client assurance that you will keep their confidential information strictly private and stored and managed in a safe manner. If clients are going to be handing you their credit card and log-in details, they need to have something which holds you to a commitment of confidentiality.

Are your clients happy?

I always ask my clients if they are happy with the service I am providing to them, this can be via a quarterly questionnaire or by talking to them directly. The method I choose to use and frequency depends on the individual client as some react differently and choose to communicate in different ways. Choose the method you think would work best as you get to know your client. The outcome of the questionnaire or call can very much depend on whether the client is being totally honest; some clients do not like to feel they are being rude or hurting your feelings, but this only serves to inhibit how you improve your service in the future. You need honest responses, so think carefully about the way you approach a client.

It's a good idea to advertise your standards clearly so that clients know what you strive for and how they can benefit from your 'meticulous planning', 'attention to detail', 'flexibility to meet the ever-changing needs of a business', 'high standards and expectations that you put on yourself' and that you are 'not just meeting their expectations but striving to surpass them'. Advertising your standards on your website is a good starting place and also set these out when you communicate with potential clients, perhaps in a proposal you send to them.

Managing your clients

I recommend keeping separate folders for each client, both on your PC's office software package and in your e-mail folders. This helps you to keep information from each client totally separate, easy to locate and easy to manage. In some client folders you may need to create sub-folders; for example, you may have a client by the name of V.A Smart, but that client may have various tasks that he requires you to do. In this case you may need to allocate one folder to 'general correspondence', one to 'documents', one to 'meeting management'. It is difficult for me to give a very comprehensive list of folder titles as the demands of clients vary significantly from one to the next. You'll need to develop a filing system that suits the needs of each of your clients.

The key to a successful working relationship with your clients is **good communication** and **efficient client management**:

- Always keep your client informed if you should be running behind schedule so that they can plan for this delay.

- If your client is reaching the end of their monthly hours allowance or retainer, send them an email to remind them and ask them if they want to top up their account.

- If you make a mistake – tell them! Truth is always the best policy and more often than not a mistake is recoverable if it is dealt with in good time. We are all human and make mistakes, but your client will be more receptive to the mistake if you own up to it promptly and honestly.

- Make a point from time to time of letting clients know how much you appreciate their custom. The small things really do matter.

- If you expect to hear from a client, but haven't, give them a call. They may have forgotten or simply have been busy, or they may not be able to identify what help they need. Your call could be just the boost they need to get back on track.

- Try and persuade clients to pay you by BACS. This is easier to manage and saves you having to run to the bank to pay in cheques.

- If for some reason it is not possible for you to get advance payment and you have to invoice your client at the end of the month, you can send letters to seek payment of over-due invoices. Start by sending a gentle reminder letter, follow this with a second reminder letter and, if after sending these you still have not been paid then you can send a 'Letter Demanding Payment' which is essentially a more formal 'final' reminder, and if this does not work, follow with a 'Letter Before Claim' (sometimes referred to as a Letter Before Action) which is a letter that sets out that the debtor (the client who owes you money) may face legal proceedings.

  If sending out a 'Letter Demanding Payment' or a 'Letter Before Claim' I would recommend sending these by post as Special Delivery. This ensures your client signs for the letter and they cannot then say the letter was not received, as you will have signed proof of delivery. Ensure you keep all records of postage and who has signed for it and when it was signed for.

  The process of debt recovery works far better, and easier, if you have a signed Client Contract in place.

- Let them know how they should send work to you.

- Inform your client of what your expected turn-around time is when carrying work out for them.

- Ask them who the main contact is to be. Find out how they would prefer you to contact them, and when. Ensure they know what is needed to get started working with them. The best way to ascertain this is by sending them a Client Assessment form.

- Remember to set your **client boundaries** – let them know when it is okay to contact you and what your working days and hours are.

- Time is money. Time management is crucial, so if your client should keep you on the phone for a long time, ensure they are aware that you will be charging them for the time you spend in conversation together, some calls can take a long time if instructions are being given and taken.

- If you are taking in-depth instructions over the telephone you may like to follow this up with an email to the client. This offers the opportunity to iron-out any misunderstanding or make any necessary changes to those instructions, if needed, before any serious work commences.

- Diarise your work with clients in blocks so that you do not forget to do something. Diarise what work you have to do, which client the work is for and add in any reminders you may need. This will help you to prioritise your workload. It will also help you to see quickly and clearly what hours you have available to take on more work. Your diary will be your best friend as you get busier with client work.

- **Don't** take on more work than you can handle. This will only serve to compromise the quality of work to your clients. Always look after your current clients first. If you do become overloaded with work, remember you can offer work to your associate virtual assistant.

- Some of your working weeks or days will be better than others. You will find some clients are more demanding than others, but you need to apply the same level of professionalism to everyone and just get on with it. It's the same for most business owners out there too.

- Always seek pre-authorisation of any expenditure. You should never surprise your client with any unexpected bills. If you have to purchase goods on their behalf ensure that they approve the costs before proceeding, preferably in writing. It is always preferable to use the credit card of your client to purchase items on their behalf. I never use my own monies to make client purchases.

- Let clients know if the work is going to take longer than expected because they are making changes to the original schedule and, if so, let them know additional costs will be incurred and what these costs will be. Again, seek authorisation for the additional costs before proceeding with the extra work.

- Remember to ask your client if there is anything you can help with. Sometimes clients do not always think of things they can delegate and so you will need to give them little 'prompts'.

- A client should never have to chase you for information or updates on progress. This should be delivered by you to the client at relevant and regular intervals.

- Start each week by looking at your diary for the following week. What work have you got to do? Is there anything you will need to order in to complete a task? Are there any travel arrangements to be made? Is there anything outstanding that may cause a delay to the progress of specific tasks?

- Your clients should always be clear on what they are paying for. What work have you done for them and how long it took to complete. I provide the client with a timesheet, which works well for me. It helps the client to understand how my charges have been calculated and offers transparency. I have never had a client question my charges.

- Outsource any work you cannot do yourself to your associate virtual assistant, but as I've said above you **must ensure** you carefully select the right person to work with.

- When solving your clients' problems, try to treat the disease rather than the symptoms. This will ensure that, in time, your client will benefit greatly from the strong foundations you have put in place for them.

- Be pro-active – try to anticipate what your client's needs may be and how you may be able to help. Sometimes clients struggle to identify what you can help with and so you need to point them in the right direction.

- When you have built a professional working relationship with clients, don't be afraid to ask them, if you feel you can, whether they know of anyone who they feel would benefit from their help. This is a good way of getting extra work for yourself.

- One further point I should mention is that you shouldn't ever allow clients to mentally or emotionally abuse you. Unfortunately, as with anything in life, this can happen but you are a professional and you should expect to be treated as such. If you give such a client a warning which then goes unheeded, then perhaps the best solution is to terminate your contract with them. You always have the right to say 'no'. Your physical and mental health are of vital importance to you and to the running of a successful business, so take good care of them both!

At source payment methods

There may be an occasion where your client may be attending an event to showcase their products or services, they may ask you to attend with them to help out. If they are selling goods at a trade show for example, they may need a way to take payments via credit or debit card from customers. The ones I have used are iZettle and Square, both are easy to use and set up and offer pay per transaction, they also integrate well into other systems. Take a look at both and familiarise yourself with that they do and how they work, you never know, a client may want you to source a system for them and they would be really impressed if you could do this quickly for them!

https://www.izettle.com/gb
https://squareup.com/gb

You will need to find out if WiFi/3G or 4G is available at the venue and if you have to pay to use their WiFi facility (some make an additional charge) as these systems will need this to work.

Transcription

You may be approached by a client to type transcriptions for them. Two of the more popular programmes for doing this are Winscribe (which is expensive, but a professional programme) and Express Scribe. There are many others available and it would be a case of you searching the web for systems that would suit your needs. I would recommend you think about how much work you may get before spending money on one of these programmes- if transcription work is going to be the main service you are offering, then you may wish to invest in one, but if it would only be occasional, then try one of the free downloads first. One of the things you would need to consider is the foot pedal, this is because not all foot pedals are compatible with all transcription software – check compatibility before you purchase.

www.winscribe.co.uk
http://www.expressscribe.co.uk/download/

Email Management

This is probably one of the hardest parts of client management to master. You will not only have to manage your own emails, but you may also have multiple email accounts for your clients to cope with too.

I open different folders in both my own and my client's email accounts to help me manage emails. I also add coloured tabs to each email so that I know what is completed, what is ongoing, what is outstanding. I move any unwanted emails to a 'junk' folder and delete them at the end of the week (I always double check them first to ensure that I have not accidentally moved an email to junk that should not be there – accidents do happen!) to keep my computer system running efficiently. Any emails that need the attention of my client I mark in red, so that they know it requires their response. The overall objective is to reduce the amount of emails your client is having to handle, while ensuring that any they need to respond to are dealt with in a timely and professional manner.

Potential Client Management

As part of client management, you will have to manage 'potential' clients too. Be prepared to deal with enquiries you receive efficiently and effectively:

- Always have a pad and pen near your phone to take down messages. You need their full name, phone/mobile number, company name, a summary of what their enquiry is about, the date and time they called and what follow-up work is required. Remember to give the caller time to let you know why they are calling without you jumping in; ask any questions you may have towards the end of the call if possible.

- Check your email inbox at frequent intervals (at least twice a day). Any enquiries via email or via your website contact form should be responded to quickly. Always follow up on any leads and diarise them accordingly.

- Keep a check on your social media platforms in the event that someone may contact you via those systems.

- Always have access to your phone to take or return calls.

- Think about advanced payment incentives and write down how you would go about persuading a potential client to pay in advance for your services.

When meeting or speaking with a potential client - be prepared:

- Take a look at their website in advance and learn as much about them and what they do as possible.

- Find out what 'pains' the potential client has and how you can help them. Read their blogs and social media posts to see what are they 'grumbling' about and consider if you have a solution you can offer to help them. Keep a record of their grumbles along with the solutions you came up with. These records will come in very useful as you develop your business.

- Type up a list of questions you want to ask the potential client during any telephone conversation or Skype call. Leave a space in-between the questions so that you can write down the answers. Prepare a client question prompt sheet.

- Once you have the information you need you can then prepare a client proposal. This should set out what has been agreed between the two of you. You can then email your proposal to them. There is no guarantee that the potential client will accept the proposal, but if this is the case do not beat yourself up about it and move on to other potential clients. No matter how big companies are, they never get all of the work they hope for. This is business and it happens everywhere.

- If you have met with the client in person and have discussed in depth what is needed, sending a proposal may not be appropriate as you may have already agreed on a way forward and have all the necessary information.

If this is the case, send them your Client Contract, which should reflect what was agreed, for them to sign off and return to you. Once they have returned the signed contract to you, you then sign and date it and provide a completed copy to your client for their own records. **Always** review your Client Contract before sending it to the potential client to double-check that nothing has been omitted. I make a point of not starting any work until the client has returned the signed contract.

There are programmes you can use that allow you to deal with the signing of documents electronically and the two I personally use are DocuSign and HelloSign.

This saves you having to scan documents. Take a look at these two programmes to see how they work.

https://www.hellosign.com/
https://go.docusign.com

Working for friends

Remember you are now a business owner. It is okay to have 'mates' rates' but your friends are now your clients when it comes to carrying out work for them and should be treated as such. It is not unheard of that friends have been taken to small claims courts for non-payment of invoiced sums. Putting my legal hat on, I can say that the amount of times I have seen the best of friends become the best of enemies over non-payment of monies owed is far too many to mention. It's extremely sad to see and I truly hope that this should never happen to you. *Always* have a written agreement with friends. Bind them to the payment of your fees and in doing so they will have greater respect for you and your professionalism, while you get the money you are owed. Let's face it, if they have the intention of paying you, then they should have no objection to putting that in writing.

PRACTICAL TASK #6

Think about 'mates' rates'. If you were to carry out work for a friend, what rate would you charge them?

Working with International Clients

Being virtual assistants means we can work with anyone in the world, the advancements in modern technology has opened the boundaries between countries and has enabled us to offer business services to almost any individual or company.

However, there are some important points you need to know about and consider when working with international clients:

- Why is it important to have a client contract when working with overseas clients?

- Which law courts have jurisdiction and why is this important?

- How should I invoice a client?

- What payment methods are there for receiving payments from overseas clients?

- What about insurance cover?

- What about VAT – how does that work with overseas clients?

Let's take a look at each bullet point in turn:

Why is it important to have a client contract when working with overseas clients?

It is important to have a client contract with all clients, whether UK or overseas, as this formalises the working agreement between you. However, when working with international clients it is important that your client contract contains governing law and jurisdiction clauses.

<u>Which law courts have jurisdiction and why is this important?</u>

A 'governing law' clause in a contract makes it clear that the terms of the contract will be governed by, and construed in accordance with, the laws of England and Wales.

A 'jurisdiction clause' makes it clear in a contract that **both** parties irrevocably agree that any disputes or claims arising out of, or in connection with, the contract the courts of England and Wales have exclusive jurisdiction. Ensure your client signs and dates <u>your</u> contract, rather than you signing theirs.

This means that, heaven forbid, should a client take you to court to make a claim, that claim will have to be heard in the law courts of England and Wales and not in the country where your client is based.

Without a contract, if your overseas client should take you to court, then it would be a very expensive ordeal because a decision would have to be made as to which country and in which court your case would be heard.   A court may use the Brussels Regulation to determine this (if your client is from an EU member state).   You may argue that the contract was performed in the UK, but your client may challenge that argument by saying that any claim should be in a court in their country. This is where it can get very messy and **very** expensive

Having a carefully considered and worded contract containing governing law and jurisdiction clauses keeps the terms of your contract UK based. This gives you peace of mind that should an overseas client take you to court, the case would be heard in a court based in the UK.

Please note that 'governing law' and 'jurisdiction' are not the same thing and both should be clearly defined in any client contract.

How should I invoice a client?

You should invoice your overseas client just as you would your UK client, however, you need to take exchange rates into account when exchanging foreign currency to £sterling. Always state your payment terms and conditions on every invoice.

What payment methods are there for receiving payments from overseas clients?

When you work with overseas clients, you want to ensure a cost-effective way to get paid. One option you have is PayPal, this has a fairly low charge for transactions. Another option you have is BACS transfer, however this can be expensive and so check with your bank to see what charges would be applied for overseas BACS transactions. A third option is to use an app called 'Transfer Wise' (this is the app I like to use – find this in the Apple app store) money transfer and use this to find out the best transfer rates and payment usually goes from your client's bank to yours within a 24 hour period. There is a fee for this service, but it is relatively small. They also have a website.
https://transferwise.com/

<u>What about insurance cover</u>?

I would never recommend you work with overseas clients without appropriate insurance. This is a big risk should your overseas client bring a claim against you.

Many insurance companies will not insure you for working with overseas clients and insurance cover can be very expensive – especially if your client is based in the USA!

One way to keep your premiums down is to have a client contract in place, as suggested above. This is because your insurers will know the contract you have with your overseas client will be governed by UK laws and heard in a UK court. The insurance company some virtual assistants use when working with overseas clients is Hiscox.
https://www.hiscox.co.uk

You do need to consider how much work you are likely to get from overseas clients – is the likely income you receive from them going to cover the additional costs of insurance cover?

<u>What about VAT – how does this work with overseas clients</u>?

Please see later in this book under the VAT section.

<u>Getting what you're worth!</u>

When I first started my business, I was determined to get paid the amount I felt I was worth, whether this was from a UK or International client. I had worked very hard to build my own skills, knowledge and experience, and made many sacrifices along the way, and so I thought to myself, "Why should I give that away cheaply?".

The best way to get the money you are worth is to make yourself an indispensable asset to your clients – you have to be worth your rates in the eyes of the client. You need to deliver a top-class service, one which makes the client think 'I cannot manage without my virtual assistant and that I need to do all I can to keep her/him'. Your client will be only too happy to tell you whether they are happy with your services. If they don't tell you, then ask. You can only improve your services if you know what needs improving in the first place.

When I take on a new client, I always let them know that I will raise my rates each year. I only raise my rates a little, this way the client gets used to the fact that my rates are going to increase each year, they can plan for that small increase in their own business plan and it does not come as such a shock to them. I find this works much better than leaving it a few years to raise your rates and then telling your client your fees are going to increase by £5(?) an hour – they find this a lot harder to accept – I personally find that small, annual increases are the best way to keep my rates at an acceptable level, from a client viewpoint.

Remember that all business owners will raise their own rates to their clients and so they should expect you to raise yours too. Prices always increase in business, e.g. utility bills, insurance and you need to keep in line with those increases, otherwise you could end up working for very little.

I always make a point of sending an email to my clients, around a month before I increase my rates, to remind them. If they have given me a 'glowing report' about my services or have written a testimonial for me, I always make a point of mentioning it in my email to them.

The sort of email I send out is something along these lines:

Dear XXX

You may recall our conversation when we began working together, when I mentioned I would raise my rates each year, I am just writing, as a matter of courtesy, to remind you that as from [Date][month] my hourly rate will be increasing from £[XX] to £[XX].

It was great [to hear you were very happy with the services I provide] [to receive the amazing testimonial you kindly wrote for me]. Knowing how highly you value what I bring to your business, and to you as the business owner, is very satisfying indeed.

I look forward to working with you going forward and taking your business to the next level

With sincere thanks,

Yours XXXX

The General Data Protection Regulations (GDPR) – A Guide

Your clients need reassurance that you are looking after and handling their private details and information properly and in accordance with the law, protecting it at all times. This comes in the form of the General Data Protection Regulations (GDPR).

In most cases, you will be handling some form of personal data – names, email addresses, home addresses, home telephone numbers, credit card details etc- both in the case of you holding your client's information and you holding your client's client information – these all fall within the scope of the Act. There may also be occasions where you are exchanging data with EU or USA clients.

As you handle personal information on a day to day basis of individuals, you have an obligation to protect that information under the GDPR.

What is GDPR?

The EU GDPR will more uniformally regulate data protection in all of Europe. The GDPR replaces the Data Protection Act (1998).

The regulation took effect on and from 25 May 2018.

Data Protection – The Main Concepts

- Transparency, fairness and Lawfulness – any personal data is to be processed in a transparent, fair and lawful manner.

- Data minimisation – any personal data collected needs to be collected for a specific purpose and must be limited to what is necessary.

- Data Accuracy – it is important to keep personal data accurate and up to date using every reasonable step to ensure any inaccurate/out of date personal data is either deleted or updated.

- Purpose limitation – personal data is only to be collected for specific legitimate purposes.

- Storage of data – data is to be kept in a form which permits identification of an individual and for no longer than is necessary and for the purpose for which it was originally collected.

- Data confidentiality and Integrity – it is important to ensure appropriate security, this includes accidental loss, damage or destruction. Measures which should be taken are to add password protection to documents containing personal information relating to clients/ employees/associates, encrypt any USB sticks used to transport data, restrict access to data folders/ directories to those individuals who **need** access to the data, e.g. those who have direct report, those who process personal identifiable data or hold identifiable information (data which can identify the person to whom the data relates).

What is different now GDPR has taken over from the Data Protection Act?

The main difference is expanded accountability, you must be able to document that all guidelines have been noted and complied with.

You will need to prove appropriate documented adherence to the principles set out below:

- Lawful processing of data (e.g. data required for…salary payments, contractual purposes)
- Data minimisation
- Data accuracy
- Purpose limitation
- Storage of data
- Data confidentiality and integrity

Get the basis right – create solid foundations

Explicit consent – you will need to have explicit consent from each individual to process their personal data (it if is for none lawful/legitimate reasons - e.g. if you require a copy of their medical records, or wish to use their photo for marketing campaigns or add their name to a marketing list).

Contract – where processing personal data is necessary for the performance of a contract and is required for lawful/legitimate reasons (e.g. salary payment, health and safety (emergency contact details), invoicing) this does not require additional or explicit consent.

Who needs to be aware

Anyone who has a direct report or processes personal data which can identify an individual.

Anyone who could hold identifiable information.

What Data should be retained (example list)

- Salary details
- Absence management records
- Contact database
- Invoice details
- Rights to Work documentation

What does this mean for individuals?

- Education and awareness – you, your employees, your associates need to be aware of GDPR.

- Culture change – as outlined above, there needs to be a change of culture with regard to collecting and storing personal data.

- Data cleanse – ensure that all data held is up to date and accurate, if you hold any marketing lists (people you send marketing emails to), you will need to write to each individual to seek their permission to be on your list. Make it **very clear** how they can unsubscribe from marketing lists, e.g. who can they contact (named person and email address), by pressing the 'unsubscribe button at the bottom/top of this newsletter').

- Requirement to report a data breach – if someone should report a data breach, steps need to be taken to report that breach. The GDPR introduces a duty on you to report certain types of personal data breach. You must do this within 72 hours of becoming aware of the breach, where feasible.

- If the breach is likely to result in a high risk of adversely affecting individuals' rights and freedoms, you must also inform those individuals without undue delay.

- You should ensure you have robust breach detection, investigation and reporting procedures in place. This will facilitate decision-making about whether or not you need to notify the Information Commissioner's Office (ICO) and the affected individuals.

- You must keep a record of any personal data breaches.

- Your clients need to know who the Data Controller is and how they report a breach. You can find details here:
  https://ico.org.uk/for-organisations/report-a-breach/personal-data-breach/

What is a personal data breach?

A personal data breach means a breach of security leading to the accidental or unlawful destruction, loss, alteration, unauthorised disclosure of, or access to, personal data. This includes breaches that are both accidental and deliberate. It also means that a breach is more than just about losing personal data.

Personal data breaches can include (but is not limited to):

- Access by unauthorised personnel

- Deliberate or accidental action (or where no action has been taken) by the Data Controller or Data Processor

- Sending personal data to an incorrect recipient

- Technology – mobile phones, PC, laptops, USB sticks etc – being stolen or lost

- Altering personal data without permission

- Loss of availability of personal data

A personal data breach can be broadly defined as a security incident that has affected the confidentiality, integrity or availability of personal data. In short, there will be a personal data breach whenever any personal data is lost, destroyed, corrupted or disclosed; if someone accesses the data or passes it on without proper authorisation; or if the data is made unavailable, for example, when it has been encrypted by ransomware, or accidentally lost or destroyed.

GDPR makes clear that when a security incident takes place, you should quickly establish whether a personal data breach has occurred and, if so, promptly take steps to address it, including telling the ICO if necessary.

What breaches do you need to notify the ICO (Information Commissioner's Office) about?

When a personal data breach has occurred, you need to establish the likelihood and severity of the resulting risk to people's rights and freedoms. If it's likely that there will be a risk then you must notify the ICO; if it's unlikely then you don't have to report it. However, if you decide you don't need to report the breach, you need to be able to justify this decision, so you should document it.

In assessing risk, it's important to focus on the potential negative consequences for individuals.

A personal data breach may, if not addressed in an appropriate and timely manner, result in a physical, material or non-material damage to individuals, such as loss of control over their personal data or limitation of their rights, discrimination, identify theft or fraud, financial loss of confidentiality of personal data protected by professional secrecy.

This in effect means that a breach can have a range of adverse effects on individuals, which include emotional distress and physical and material damage. Some personal data breaches will not lead to risks beyond possible inconvenience to those who need the data to do their job. Other breaches can significantly affect individuals whose personal data has been compromised. You need to assess this case by case, looking at all relevant factors.

On becoming aware of a breach, you should try to contain it and assess the potential adverse consequences for individuals, based on how serious or substantial these are, and how likely they are to happen.

What role do Data Processors have?

If you are to designate a Data Processor, and this processor suffers a breach, then they must inform the Data Controller without undue delay as soon as it becomes aware and the Data Controller will then assess whether it should inform the ICO of the breach.

What does a breach notification to the Data Controller need to contain?

When reporting a breach, the GDPR says you must provide a description of the nature of the personal data breach including, where possible:

- the categories and approximate number of individuals concerned;

- the categories and approximate number of personal data records concerned;

- the name and contact details of the Data Controller

- a description of the likely consequences of the personal data breach; and

- a description of the measures taken, or proposed to be taken, to deal with the personal data breach, including, where appropriate, the measures taken to lessen any possible adverse effects.

What if you do not have all the required information available as yet?

The GDPR recognises that it will not always be possible to investigate a breach fully within 72 hours to understand exactly what has happened and what needs to be done to resolve the issue. The GDPR allows you to provide the required information in phases, as long as this is done without undue further delay.

However, the GDPR expect Data Controllers to prioritise the investigation, give it adequate resources, and deal with the breach as a matter of urgency. You must still notify the ICO of the breach when you become aware of it and submit further information as soon as possible. If you know you won't be able to provide full details within 72 hours, it is a good idea to explain the delay to the ICO and tell them when you expect to submit further information.

When do you need to tell an individual(s) about a breach?

If a breach is likely to result in a high risk to the rights and freedoms of individuals, the GDPR says you must inform those concerned directly and without undue delay. In other words, this should take place as soon as possible.

If you decide not to notify individuals, you will still need to notify the ICO unless you can demonstrate that the breach is unlikely to result in a risk to an individual's rights and freedoms. You should also remember that the ICO has the power to compel you to inform affected individuals if they consider there is a high risk. You should document your decision-making process.

What information must you provide to individuals when telling them about a breach?

You need to describe, in clear and plain language, the nature of the personal data breach and, at least:

- the name and contact details of the Data Controller

- a description of the likely consequences of the personal data breach; and

- a description of the measures taken, or proposed to be taken, to deal with the personal data breach and including, where appropriate, the measures taken to lessen any possible adverse effects.

Does the GDPR require you to take any other steps in response to a breach?

You should ensure that you record all breaches, regardless of whether or not they need to be reported to the ICO.

As with any security incident, you should investigate whether or not the breach was a result of human error or an internal process issue and look into how a recurrence can be prevented, whether this is through better processes, further training or other corrective steps.

What happens if you fail to notify?

Failing to notify a breach when required to do so can result in a significant fine. The fine can be combined with the ICO's other corrective powers. It is important to make sure you have a robust breach-reporting process in place to ensure you detect and can notify a breach, on time; and to provide the necessary details.

What can go Wrong?

Accidents do happen! It is so easy when you are under a lot of pressure to send an email to the wrong person that contains personal data (this is why it is important to password protect sensitive email attachments). Send the password for the document(s) separately. Hackers could attack your system with Malware, Ransomware and Spyware, keeping your IT equipment and internal processes secure and robust is vital to ensuring no breaches occur!

What is classed as personal data?

There are 6 questions you need to ask yourself to assess whether processing of data is compliant

1.   Is the data about a person or people?

2.   What is the purpose for collecting the data? Do you really need it?

3.   What is the legal basis (e.g. to pay salaries, health and safety, invoicing for work undertaken as part of a

contract) for collecting/holding the data. There has to be a lawful basis

4.   Is the data being held and/or transferred securely?

5.   How long will you keep the data? What is the deletion date?

6.   Is this process already documented?

1.   <u>Is the data about a person or people?</u>

These are examples of personal data:

- Name
- Payroll/salary details
- Date of Birth
- Email address (including business email where the individuals name is given)
- Personal ID number
- Travel details
- Absence management details
- Religious beliefs
- Health records
- Criminal records
- Trade Union membership

These are examples of what is <u>not</u> classed as personal data:

- Generic email addresses (e.g. inf@joebloggs.com)
- Marketing budget
- Generic analysis data
- Generic research data

2. What is the purpose for collecting data and do you really need it?

- You need to have a specific reason for collecting or holding personal data. You will need to be very clear about why you need it.

- You need to ensure that data will only be processed by you for a legitimate reason.

3. What is the lawful basis (e.g. to pay salaries, health and safety) for collecting/holding the data. There has to be one

- You need to ensure there is a lawful basis for every personal data processing carried out.

- A person can give consent to process their data. This consent has to be given freely and can be withdrawn at any time.

The processing of personal data is in the best interests of the individual but common sense must prevail in certain situations, such as an accident occurring at work. For example, if someone's life was at risk, then data protection privacy would be secondary to saving an individual's life. In these circumstances you would provide the emergency services with the necessary individual's details. You would have a right to do this.

4. Is the data being held and/or transferred securely?

- If you use a USB stick then ensure it is encrypted

- If you are transferring the data (e.g emailing personal data to a colleague) does the document being transferred need to be password protected?

- Does your phone have a locking code or other security access feature?

- Does your PC/laptop have secure password protection

- In certain instances, it may be better to share a link to a shared folder rather than attaching files

- Always ask yourself "Is this data being protected in an adequate way"?

With the world we live in today where data is transferred from one person to another very quickly and easily, with GDPR everyone has a responsibility to be compliant and one of the questions to ask yourself if this "How would I want my personal data to be treated"? GDPR is mostly about common sense and being aware of the potential dangers of transferring and holding personal data and the consequences of not doing this in the correct way. One of the best ways to transfer data is by shared drives or folders.

5.   How long will you keep the data? What is the deletion date?

When you are collecting personal data you need to decide on the length of time you are going to keep it and when and how you are going to destroy any redundant data. Remember, under GDPR you can only keep data for as long as is necessary. Ensure you let your client know if you are going to delete any personal data – especially ex-clients, to ensure they have what they need before deleting.

6.   Is this process already documented?

A data cleanse must be undertaken to ensure that only relevant and current up to date personal data is kept and a review date set for each [year/month/quarter] to ensure this process is repeated to ensure all personal data records are kept in line with GDPR guidelines.

This includes any ex-client documentation, if you are still holding personal data of ex-clients then it should be securely destroyed – unless there is a specific reason to keep the data, in which case it should be documented that a 'data cleanse took place on [   ] and X,Y,Z personal data was destroyed by [name of who destroyed it].   X,Y,Z personal data was kept because [give reasons as to why the data was kept – remember it has to be a lawful reason].   Keep these data cleanse records up to date and stored securely.

Check list – what you should check during a data cleanse:

- Emails, saved emails, folders storing emails – delete any emails that contain client/employee/associate personal data unless there is a specific reason or retaining it.

- Check desk drawers, filing cabinets, document trays etc – destroy all personal data that is (1) out of date (2) you should not have in your possession (only designated personnel must hold personal data).

- Clients/staff/associates need to know who to hand documentation to for destruction and details of the destruction to be documented

<u>You/all staff</u> in all departments/your associates/your clients will be responsible for compliance

7. Personal Data of Children

Children need particular protection when you are collecting and processing their personal data because they may be less aware of the risks involved.

If you process children's personal data then you should think about the need to protect them and design your systems and processes with this in mind.

You need to have a lawful basis for processing a child's personal data. Consent is one possible lawful basis for processing, but it is not the only one.

If you are relying on consent as your lawful basis for processing, when offering an online service directly to a child, in the UK only children aged 13 or over are able provide their own consent.

For children under this age you need to get consent from whoever holds parental responsibility for the child - unless the online service you offer is a preventive or counselling service.

Children need specific protection when you use their personal data for marketing purposes or creating personality or user profiles.

So what does all this mean in general terms?

Under the GDPR there are two main descriptions you need to be aware of:

Data Controller

This is the person (whether it be alone, jointly or in common with other people) who determines the purposes for and manner in which personal data is to be processed.

Data Processor

This is the person, in relation to personal data (other than employees of the Data Controller) who process the data on behalf of the Data Controller.

One of the main changes the GDPR has introduced in relation to data management is to make virtual assistants responsible for the data they process on behalf of their clients and so it is important you know and understand the source of any data you are handling and how service providers are storing it on your behalf.

What steps need to be taken?

You (and indeed your client, if they are holding and managing data of their own and your associate virtual assistant) will need to ensure you register with the ICO as the Data Controller. You can register with the Information Commissioner's office for the purpose of GDPR here:
https://ico.org.uk/for-organisations/register/

1. As the Data Controller you must ensure these new regulations are complied with.

2. You will need to let your clients know who the Data Controller is when communicating with them. If you

are managing and storing their data, then you are responsible for it.

3. You will need to inform people who will have access to their data and what they have signed up for.

4. I would suggest you add the name of the Data Controller and details of how you store, manage and handle personal data to your website Privacy Policy.

5. You need to be sure where your client got the data they are using to communicate with their clients, it could be a mailing list they have given you to send out a mailshot on their behalf, where did that list come from? How did people get on their list in the first place? Did they subscribe knowing what they were going to receive? Ensure you have your client's response in writing and keep a copy of it.

6. You will need to have direct consent to add people to a mailing list/marketing communication. It will no longer be acceptable to 'assume' consent.

7. Keep the data you store under review, only keep it for as long as you need to minimise the risks of a data breach. It is so easy to let data build up over a period of many years. Review your PC, mobile (a lot of people forget they have data stored on there too!), laptop, USB stick/flash drive, external hard drive, online apps and programmes, Dropbox etc. These are all places where you store information.

8. The new GDPR rules state that you must deal with 'unsubscribe' requests quickly. You will also need to

inform people how their information is stored. I would recommend thinking about your website Privacy Policy in this regard and ensuring it contains a section on how the information of visitors to your website is stored and managed.

9. People need to know who is responsible for handling their data (the name of the Data Controller), how they should contact that person - ensure you add your email address as well as clear instructions on how they can unsubscribe should they wish to. This information should be added to all and each marketing communication.

10. It has always been best practice to include an 'unsubscribe' option on all marketing emails and a dual 'opt-in' option – this is where people fill in their email address on a website and then receive a confirmation email. Under the new GDPR you are under a legal obligation to comply with unsubscribe requests.

11. Keep copies of any emails, event attendance sheets, website newsletter 'sign up' forms etc – all relevant documentary evidence where people have 'explicitly' given you permission to send them marketing information.

12. The GDPR will restrict the transfer of data outside of the EU, unless an international organisation can demonstrate they have a satisfactory level of protection and can handle data appropriately, this not only relates to marketing lists but also social media log in details, your on-line accountancy software (where billing etc details are stored), where is your data

backup being held and what security measures are in place to safeguard that information. If you are not sure, ask, and keep a copy of their response – be prepared to move your back-up storage facility elsewhere if you are dissatisfied with how data is safeguarded.

13.   If your client is outside of the EU, ask them if they are signed up to the EU-USA Privacy Shield, this is a framework that covers exchanges of personal data between the EU and the United States. Ask them for a copy of their policy.
       https://www.privacyshield.gov/welcome

14.   You will need to have clear reporting procedures for any data breaches that may occur and these should be documented. You are under an obligation to report any breach as quickly as possible, and within 72 hours after becoming aware of any breach to the ICO and the people who are affected.

15.   You must inform clients without delay if there has been a breach (and within 72 hours). You need to think about who and how you are going to contact your clients if a breach should occur.

GDPR and Your Website

With GDPR there are also a few things you need to do/consider where your website is concerned:

1.   You may want to consider an SSL Certificate, this puts a picture of a padlock on the URL of your website, so that people know it is a secure site. I believe Google

are going to give preference to these sites over those who don't have them. What this means is, if you do not have an SSL certificate, when someone searches for, example, 'virtual assistants in Birmingham' using the Google search engine, Google will list all those virtual assistant websites that have the secure SSL certificate in the search result listings above those who do not have one. SSL ensures that all data is encrypted when being sent via your website to you, e.g via a newsletter sign up or your website contact form.

2. Ensure you add a Privacy Policy to your website a mentioned earlier, this needs to include how you will collect and handle the data of visitors to your website and also include details regarding Cookies. You may like to take a look at the one I have on my website for guidance.
    https://www.wrightbusinesssupportcentre.co.uk/privacy-policy

3. Anonymise the IP address within the analytics Java Scrips code. This just basically hides the IP address of visitors to your website.

Internet/PC Security and Back-Up

The GDPR extends to security of files. If you have sensitive files that contain many addresses, emails, telephone numbers etc, it is always a good idea to protect them with a password or encrypt them.

There have been many occasions where people of have left laptops on trains and buses, where people view data on a laptop while travelling on a train where the person sitting next to them can see, there have been occasions where people have left USB sticks at meetings or left it on a train - always ensure you password protect laptops, mobile phones, USB sticks etc, anything that carries and stores data, for security reasons.

Many businesses have suffered over the years with 'cyber attacks' – 'Malware'/'Ransomware' – and chances are you have seen or heard about these sorts of attack in the press or on TV, but what exactly are they? Let's take a look!

'Malware' is a basically malicious software. It is specifically designed to cause harm to data and devices. These are commonly known as viruses, spyware and trojans.

'Ransomware' - these land on your system in various formats – it could be from a website that you click on or a document that you download. This type of 'virus' copies all the files on your computer, it then encrypts those copied files and deletes the originals that you originally created. Once this happens, it is a **major** inconvenience in terms of money and time.

There are three options open to you (1) you can pay the ransom – which tends to become more expensive each day that you do not pay the ransom to retrieve your files however there is no guarantee that you will get your files back and even if you do, there is still the problem of you having the 'bug' on your PC – also by paying a ransom you are encouraging this kind of activity (2) you can pay an IT technician to see if they can help you to retrieve the files for you – but there are no guarantees your files can be retrieved and this can prove very expensive (3) just delete everything on your computer – restore it to factory settings – and start from scratch.

The best way to avoid Malware and Ransomware attacking your PC/laptop is to ensure you install appropriate internet security. I personally use Sophos but there are others available and some of the more popular programmes are:

https://www.mcafee.com
https://www.sophos.com
http://symantec-norton.com
https://www.kaspersky.co.uk/

Take a look at the above to see what they offer, many have special offers on and so shop around – but do not compromise on quality – it is worth paying that bit more for very good internet/PC security.

Hard drive back up and disaster recovery

I have an external hard drive and small business server which I use for backing up my systems at the end of each day. I personally don't like to rely solely on my PC or laptop hard drive for storage. As your client base grows you will be storing more and more information on your PC or laptop and you need to ensure that you have a disaster recovery system in place should you need to use it. It is always best to have a back-up off-site too. If, heaven forbid, you should be on the receiving end of a 'cyber attack', you will at least be able to retrieve your files from your cloud account, e.g. Drobox.

<u>Insurance</u>

You, as a business owner, also require various forms of reassurance that your business is protected against as many eventualities as possible. Insurance cover is essential to any business, and can give you the reassurance you need when working for yourself. We all hope we never have to use it, but it gives peace of mind to know it is there in an emergency.

There are many types of insurance cover for home working, professional indemnity, public liability, car, home office contents, health and income. I have listed the main ones below, you may already have signed up to some of these insurance policies, but you may have to notify your insurance broker/policy provider to let them know that you are working from home and you need business cover.

Professional Indemnity Insurance

This covers you and your business in the event of error or omission. If a client should place a claim against you for any loss of income due to an error or omission on your part, you will need to ensure that you have the appropriate level of insurance to cover the claim made against you. An insurance broker would be able to advise you on the best cover for your business.

Public Liability

This protects you if clients suffer personal injury because of your business. It covers the costs of subsequent legal expenses or compensation claims and is an integral cover for businesses that interact regularly with clients. It also covers you for working from home and on-site with clients.

Car Insurance

If you are going to use your car for work it will need to be insured for business purposes, even if you are working from home. Whether you are attending networking events, training sessions or even meetings with potential clients for a coffee, this will be classed as 'business use' and will need to be declared with your insurer. When I insured my car for business use the insurance premium only increased by £30 per annum. A small price to pay for peace of mind and the appropriate level of insurance protection.

Contents Insurance

It's likely that your equipment, printer, laptop, PC and so on are covered under your existing home contents insurance but remember, you are now running a business and your insurance cover may need to be extended to cover business use. Speak with your current home contents insurance provider and explain to them that you are thinking of working from home and you would like to know if an additional premium for home working is required.

Health Insurance

It could be that you are leaving a company who provided private healthcare for its employees. If this is the case then you may want to approach a few private healthcare providers for quotes so that you can continue to receive this type of benefit. Be mindful that many private healthcare providers often give you big reductions on the first year of your premium, so be sure to ask them what the monthly cost would be for the second and consecutive years. I would also recommend asking them about any restrictions they may have on providing the private health cover to you.

Income Insurance

Working in a self-employed environment means you no longer have access to sick pay. Your associate virtual assistants can cover for you during holidays and short period of illness, but long term sickness is a different thing entirely. What would happen if, god forbid, you break a leg or have to have surgery which means spending many weeks unable to work? In this case, income insurance is very important as it can help you to pay your mortgage and bills.

This insurance is one of the first policies I took out when I became a virtual assistant and decided to go self-employed on a full-time basis. Thankfully I've never had to make a claim, but it is really reassuring to know it is there if I need it.

PRACTICAL TASK #7

Using the guide above, think about the forms of insurance cover that you already have in place and make a note of any which may need to be changed for business purposes, along with any new ones you think you may need to take out to ensure that you are appropriately covered.

PART 2 - FINANCES

Cashflow Projections

Your Business Plan (covered earlier in this book) will be essential in helping you to formulate your cash flow forecast. Understanding your cashflow is essential – it's all about what you have coming in and what you have going out. This projection will help you to see what you need to charge to cover your living and business expenses. If you are intending to start your business alongside a full-time employed role, you may want to create two cashflow charts: one for 5 to 9 working and one for your full-time role. This forecast will help you to decide whether going to full time straight away is right for you. These forecasts will also help you to decide if your intended rate per hour is correct and feasible. Creating a budget will help you to minimise financial risks.

Bear in mind that it could take a while to get your first client secured if you are starting from scratch, so it is a good idea to plan for this. I'd allow around three to four months as a contingency. You may of course be lucky enough to get one or more clients much sooner than this and if you do, fantastic! If not, then at least you have a back-up plan in place. The first client will come along, it is just a matter of when!

How Much Should You Charge?

When you are starting a business one of the more difficult tasks is knowing what to charge. This is where your business plan comes in useful. You will need to know what your overheads are: do you have a mortgage to pay? How much is your rent? What are your monthly outgoings? Do they include insurance fees, utility costs, office equipment and childcare? You will need to work out what your outgoings are and ensure that your incomings can better them.

Work out what you need to earn and divide this by the number of hours you have available to work. It's important to remember that you need to leave time to do your own admin and marketing. When I first started my business I completely underestimated how much time this would take. I left at least one day per week to do this, which I found to be sufficient at the beginning, but it may work out differently for you.

Per Hour Rates

The average hourly rate for a virtual assistant may be dependent on where you live. If you live in London the living costs are higher and so the rates may be higher too. The rate is also dependent on what services you're offering. If you have very specialist knowledge you can charge a higher rate. Charging very low rates will only serve to send clients the wrong message. You want them to take you seriously and feel they can trust you and your professionalism, so if you charge a very low rate it can send out a negative signal. Can you make a decent living if charging low rates? The standard rate for a virtual assistant in the UK is £25 per hour.

Retainer Rates

If you can get a client on a retainer, then great. A retainer is made up of a specific amount of hours each month for a set fee. If the client does not use those hours by the month's end, then generally they would be lost or you could carry a certain number of hours to the following month. I personally only allow 2 hours carry over and if the client does not use them, I still charge for them and the client then loses those hours – I do not carry them over a second time to ensure that hours do not build up and become unmanageable. I personally do charge a little less than my hourly rate for retainers, this is because (1) if I am guaranteed a certain amount of hours per month, I do not have to pay to advertise, I do not need to attend as many networking events to find work to fill those hours (2) as I always seek payment in advance for all retainer work and ask for a three month notice period in writing should they wish to terminate the arrangement (I include this in my client contract) - I have surety of income (3) it ensures the client gets a good deal to encourage continued custom. That said, I do know virtual assistants who do not offer a lower retainer rate as they feel the client is benefiting from exclusive use of their time. This is really about your personal preference and how you wish to work.

I would usually ask my client to set up a Standing Order or regular monthly payment via BACS to ensure I receive payment in advance for retainers.

Project Rates

As well as retainer rates, I also offer project rates. I work out the amount of hours I feel a project will take and charge this figure to the client. I always ensure that the project price does not come below my standard hourly rate. When negotiating a project price I always make the client aware that if the project takes longer than expected due to client changes or failure to deliver the information I need, then the project price may increase. I do not advertise my project rates on my website as the price is very much dependent on what the project involves. Instead, I negotiate each project on a case by case basis. For small projects £1,000 or less, I charge 50% in advance and 50% on completion. For larger projects £1,000 and over, I charge 50% in advance, 25% in the middle and 25% on completion. This ensures I keep receiving income while the project is ongoing.

When working on projects I <u>always</u> have a client contract in place that contains a clause for abortive costs, as well as many other clauses, that ensure I am paid should the scope of the project change and it take longer than expected to complete due to the client changing their mind or asking for additions or if they decide to abort the work at no fault of mine. Sometimes these can be large amounts and need to be covered in a contract.

Day Rates

I do offer day rates, some clients prefer me to work on site and for the whole day – this may be because I may need to use their on-site systems or work with one of their own team members or part of my working arrangements may include covering their reception.

If I am travelling to the client for the whole day I do not charge less than my hourly rate for the length of time I am there, so based on the standard hourly virtual assistant per hour rate of £25 as an example, if I worked at the client's premises for 8 hours, I would charge £200 per day. However, as my clients are local I do not charge them travel time and travel expenses – as I would do if I was only visiting them for a few hours during the day.

What I offer to clients when working with them for a full day at their premises is 'business continuity' and clients are prepared to pay for this level of service as it is very beneficial to their business.

Free Trials

I know of some virtual assistants who have offered free trials. Personally, I would not recommend this for the simple reason that if a client has a job that will take, say, three hours (remember this could be just a one-off job!) and you do it as part of a free trial, it may transpire that you do not get any further work from them, and so you have done three hours work for no return. Word spreads quickly in the business world and if others hear of your 'free trial' you could find yourself being a very busy fool (as the old saying goes). If you're thinking of offering a free trial, just bear this in mind before considering how you would introduce your free trial and what restrictions you should apply.

Introductory Rates

You may like to offer an introductory rate to clients. If you do this, ensure that you put a time limit on how long this rate is available for and what the rate will be after the introductory period has elapsed. It is important that you do not leave yourself open to working for a cheaper rate indefinitely as this would have a negative impact on your cash flow and restrict the growth and development of your business.

Charitable Organisation Rates

I do offer reduced rates for local charitable organisations, this is my personal choice as I like to feel that I am contributing to my local community and helping those who need it. Also, charitable organisations rely on contributions to carry out the work they do. I only introduced this rate when I was more established and could afford to contribute something.

Package Prices

I personally do not offer package prices, but this is only because this is not suitable for the type of services I provide.

Many virtual assistants will put services into packages, e.g a social media package – they will offer, for example, a certain amount of hours for posting on their clients social media platforms and creating the content. This would form a package at a set price. Package prices vary dependent on what is being offered.

PRACTICAL TASK #8

Take a look at some virtual assistant websites to see how they charge for packages. How much do they cost? What do they include? How do they compare to what you are thinking of offering? It may help give you some guidance and 'food for thought' when creating your own packages. Please do not copy the content from other virtual assistant websites.

Business Loans/Support

We all need help now and again and financial assistance is no exception. It may be that you need a loan to help you get started or to undertake training, so here are a few organisations that you may find helpful in finding the funding you need with affordable repayments (where applicable).

https://www.princes-trust.org.uk/
https://www.fundingcircle.com/uk/small-business-loans/
http://nbv.co.uk/growing-a-business/grant-for-enterprise/

Your Business Accounts

It's never a good idea to mix your business finances and your personal finances. Set up a business account: this will save you from a lot of problems later as you grow your business. Many banks offer free banking for a period of 1 to 2 two years.

Did you know that you can offset your travel costs against tax under an HMRC (HM Revenue & Customs) scheme? You can offset around 45p for each business mile you make, if it is for business purposes and you are using your own car. You can include visits to your client, collecting parcels/stationery or post on behalf of your client, taking any payments into the bank, attending networking events and training. Don't forget to include the return trips as these miles are all business related too.

I would recommend keeping a separate document to log your business miles. I created an Excel document to do this. It is very simple to use and there are no subscription fees to pay and this makes it an ideal way to begin keeping accounting records. Just remember that they <u>do</u> have to be business related. Dropping the kids off at school is a no-no!

Other payments you can put through your accounts, as genuine business expenses, include parking fees, train and bus travel, reasonable subsistence (your lunch or tea if you should be working on site with a client) your own office stationery, any equipment you may need to purchase, e.g.

printer, office furniture. This is not a fixed list, but it will give you an idea of what you can record.

Remember to keep your copy invoices and all of your receipts. This is vitally important for good accounts management and in the event HMRC should wish to carry out an inspection of your accounts.

If you are working from home you can put a percentage of the cost for shared heating, lighting, broadband through your accounts as genuine business expenses. You can find more information here:
https://www.gov.uk/simpler-income-tax-simplified-expenses/working-from-home

Be aware that if you use a room in your home 'exclusively' for business, this could reduce the Capital Gains Tax private resident exemption when you sell your property. This is because any part of your home that is used solely for business will not qualify for Capital Gains Tax private residence relief.

Take a look at HMRC's online business manual for more information:
https://www.gov.uk/hmrc-internal-manuals/capital-gains-manual/cg64660

It is also worth taking a look at some of the examples they give:
https://www.gov.uk/hmrc-internal-manuals/business-income-manual/bim47825

You can find other useful information for specific deductions when using your home for business here:
https://www.gov.uk/hmrc-internal-manuals/business-income-manual/bim47800

As my business grew I changed from using an Excel spreadsheet to a cloud based accountancy system. There is usually a charge for using this software and many offer free trials. That said, it does help me to create invoices, keep track of payments, view my profit and loss accounts and print off reports. I did not change to this system until I had several clients on my books and knew I could afford the monthly subscription. When I first started out I kept a simple spreadsheet, which did the job perfectly well.

PRACTICAL TASK #9

Phone three banks and make an appointment to speak to them. Find out what they are offering to businesses and what you would need to provide them with to qualify for free banking. After your free banking period ends, your bank will then begin to make charges for your transactions and so, when your free period is nearing its end, speak to your bank and find out what the current charges will be. Don't leave it until the last minute! It is likely your bank will contact you in any event, but put a note in your diary to contact them, just in case. Remember you can always switch banks if you do not feel you are getting a good deal.

Take a brief look at some on-line accounting systems. Sage, Quickbooks and Xero are the more commonly used ones. There are a few free ones on the market but if you decide to use these bear in mind the security of your information, the level of support available and how long these systems may be around for.

When you are ready and have several clients on your books, perhaps sign up for one or more of the above on a free trial and take a look at what it does and how it looks and if you feel 'comfortable' with it.

https://shop.sage.co.uk/sageoneaccounting.aspx
http://www.intuit.co.uk/
https://www.xero.com

What your client should expect to pay for

When working with clients I always make clients aware that they will need to pay for any items I purchase or costs I incur on their behalf in addition to my rates. I would always recommend using the direct payment method of your client, e.g. their credit card, when making purchases or bookings on their behalf, this ensures you do not build up costs on behalf of your client.

Some of the items I charge to the client are:

- Stationery and postage
- Travel time and expenses
- Telephone calls
- Travel and accommodation
- Photocopying
- Printing and paper

With regard to photocopying, I would normally take bulk copying to a print shop and charge the client for my time taken to do the copying along with my travel time and expenses – and of course the cost of the photocopying itself. Where possible I charge the actual cost of copying directly to my client – I open an account with the print shop and they invoice the client direct for the printing, I just invoice for my time and travel.

For smaller requests I print the papers and pro-rata the costs of my paper and printer cartridges, remembering to add a little to cover the wear and tear of my printer, as at some point it may need to be replaced or repaired. If you are printing documents in duplex (back to back) then remember to double the cost of your printing accordingly. Remember to add to your invoice the time it takes you to do the printing!

Remember to keep a copy of any receipts for your accountancy records.

Invoicing your Client

When creating an invoice to send to your client it will need to contain certain information:

- An invoice number
- The date the invoice is created
- The date when payment has to be made
- Your payments terms (e.g payment by return, payment within 7 days from the date of invoice)
- Your bank account details
- VAT number (if applicable)
- VAT amount charged at 20%
- A description of what work has been done
- The number of hours charged
- Invoice total
- Your company name, address, email, telephone number, website address
- Your client's name and contact details
- Your logo
- Who cheques should be made payable to
- Late payment conditions (e.g. Invoices unpaid after 7 days may be subject to a late payment fee of 8% plus the Bank of England base rate. A new invoice will be issued to include the late payment fee every 7 days the payment remains overdue).

Send the original invoice and any relevant receipts to your client and keep copies for yourself. I personally always like to write on my invoices the date they were paid and by what method, e.g cheque, BACS. When I know they have been paid, I then file them with my accounts papers.

Remember – wherever possible, always try to charge items direct to your client using their credit card/account.

If you are paying for goods and then charging your clients via your invoice, you need to keep the original receipts and send copies to your client.

If your client is paying direct, e.g via their credit card, then they will need the original receipt for their accountancy records and you just keep a copy for your own records. This includes receipts for items that you may buy on the internet on their behalf, e.g from their Amazon account, you may need to print off the invoice/receipt for your client – unless they want to do this themselves.

Investing in your business

Speaking from personal experience I would always recommend investing in your business as much as you possibly can. This does not necessary mean that it has to be a lot of money, or indeed money at all, investing in your business can also mean 'time'. You will be rewarded for your efforts at a later date.

With so much available on the internet these days for free you need to be cautious when using these free resources. Some will be very good, some not so good, for example, client contracts. This is because (1) they need to be carefully written and considered (2) you need to be sure that contracts are up to date with current UK laws and regulations (3) contracts are tailored to your needs (4) that the contract you are using is applicable in the UK – other countries have different laws, rules and regulations to the UK and so any contract needs to be UK centric. Using a contract that you may have taken off the internet for free may not meet the required criteria.

VAT – How does it work? Who can register? Should I register?

The subject of VAT often crops up in social media and I am often asked by newbies to business at networking events if I can unravel the mysteries that surround VAT – some of the questions I am often asked are 'Do they have to register? "How do they register" and 'How does it work'?

I wish I could say that it is simple and quick to answer all of these questions, but I am afraid it is not as simple as it sounds! However, I will try and give you some basic information which will give you a little guidance and put you on the right path to understanding VAT.

There are a few things to consider when thinking about registering for VAT, for example:

1. What services or products are you offering, who to and why is this important to potential clients?

2. Do your products or services incur the standard 20% rate, do they come under the 'Exempt/Zero' rate or does the reduced '5%' rate apply?

3. VAT registration - Should you register for VAT? Would it be right for you and your business?

4. Do you want to register yourself and complete your own VAT returns or would you prefer to engage the services of a qualified and experienced accountant?

5. Are there different VAT rules when working with International Clients?

6. Seeking professional advice!

Let's take a closer look at the above....

1. **What services or products are you offering, who to and why is this important to potential clients?**

    Think carefully about the services you are going to offer, are they primarily aimed at, for example, charitable organisations or micro businesses (one-man bands or up to 5 employees)? The reason this is important is, if you are thinking of voluntarily registering for VAT, that many small charitable organisations and micro businesses will not be VAT registered and if you were to voluntarily register for VAT this could make you an 'unattractive' proposition for any potential clients.

    If you are VAT registered, you will be under an obligation by HMRC (HM Revenue and Customs) to charge VAT on the work you have undertaken on behalf of your client when you invoice them. Let's take a look at the difference between a VAT registered client and a none VAT registered client to see what the difference is....

    None VAT registered client

    If your client is <u>not</u> VAT registered this means they <u>will not</u> be able to offset the VAT you have charged to them against their own VAT purchases. For example, let's say you are going to invoice your client for £200 plus VAT at 20% for work you have carried out for them, this would equate to a grand invoice total of £240. As your client **is not** VAT registered they would have to pay the whole of the £240 because they **cannot** offset the £40 VAT charge. In this case, the cost to your client would be **£240.**

VAT registered client

If your client **is** VAT registered this means they **will** be able to offset the VAT you have charged to them against their own VAT purchases. For example, let's say you are going to invoice your client for £200 plus VAT at 20% for work you have carried out for them, this would equate to a grand invoice total of £240 (just as your none VAT registered client). As your client **is** VAT registered they would not, in effect, have to pay the whole of the £240. In this case, the cost to your client would be £200 (as they would offset the £40 VAT charge from HMRC against their own purchases).

As you can see from the above, there is a £40 payment difference between the none VAT registered client and the VAT registered client. The above, of course, is purely an example, but what if you were invoicing your client £2,000 plus VAT at 20%? The difference would then be £400. That is a big difference!

Whether your client is VAT registered or not does not make a difference to the way you invoice them, you would still invoice them inclusive of VAT (if of course you are VAT registered). What does make a difference is whether or not your client can offset the VAT against their own purchases. Registering for VAT is not a decision that should be taken lightly.

2. **Do your products or services incur the standard 20% rate, do they come under the 'Exempt/Zero' rate or does the reduced '5%' rate apply?**

If you are registered for VAT you must charge VAT to your clients.

There are different rates of VAT and these are:

Standard 20% - this is for most goods and services

Reduced rate 5% - some goods and services, e.g. home energy

Zero rate 0% - zero rated goods and services, e.g children's clothes, some books, food

Exempt – this applies to, for example, postage stamps.

In your case, it is highly likely you will be charging VAT to your clients at the standard rate of 20%.

3. **VAT registration - Should you register for VAT? Would it be right for you and your business**?

   You <u>must</u> register for VAT with HM Revenue and Customs (HMRC) if your business' VAT taxable turnover is more than £85,000.

   When you register, HMRC will send you a VAT registration certificate. This will confirm:

   - your VAT number

   - when you will need to submit your first VAT Return and pay any VAT liability

   - your 'effective date of registration' - this is the date you went over the threshold, or the date you voluntary registered

     You can register voluntarily if your turnover is less than £85,000, unless everything you sell is exempt. At this point, I would like to remind you of the examples I gave above regarding VAT and none VAT registered clients and to give voluntary registration careful consideration before proceeding. If you register for VAT you will have certain responsibilities to take on board and I set out below some examples:

From the effective date of registration you must:

- charge the correct amount of VAT

- pay any VAT liability due to HMRC and on time

- submit VAT returns at quarterly intervals

- keep good and clear VAT records and a VAT account

You can also offset the VAT you've paid on certain purchases made before you registered.

While you wait for your registration to come through

You are not allowed to charge or show VAT on your invoices until you receive your VAT number from HMRC. However, you will still have to pay the VAT to due to HMRC for this period.

I would suggest you increase your prices to allow for the VAT and let your clients know why. Once you have your VAT number you can then reissue your invoices showing the VAT.

How to register

Most businesses can register online at:
https://online.hmrc.gov.uk/registration/newbusiness/business-allowed.

By doing this you will (1) register for VAT and (2) create an online VAT account (sometimes called a 'Government Gateway account'). You will need this account if you are going to submit your own VAT Returns to HMRC. You will need your VAT number to create your account.

Getting your VAT registration certificate

You should get your VAT registration certificate within 14 working days, though it can take longer. This can either be sent to your VAT online account or by post.

What you need to provide

You will need to provide details such as your turnover, what your business activity is and your bank account details. Your VAT registration date is known as your 'effective date of registration'. You will have to pay HMRC any VAT due from this date. You can register for VAT yourself, you do not need to ask an accountant to do this for you, unless you want to.

So...how does VAT work?

You can only charge VAT if your business is registered for VAT.

The VAT you would charge would likely be on the goods and services you sell to your client or associate virtual assistant.

These are known as 'taxable supplies'. There are different rules for charities.

You may reclaim VAT you have paid to others for goods or services.

You will need to submit a VAT return to HMRC every quarter (3 months).

If you have charged more VAT (for the goods and services you have supplied) than you have paid (for the goods or services you have purchased from others), you will need to pay the difference to HMRC or you can claim the difference back from HMRC if you have paid more VAT than you have charged.

<u>Including and Excluding VAT</u>

You will need to calculate, when charging VAT on your goods or services or when working out the amount of VAT you can claim back, here is a simple way to calculate:

Price inclusive of VAT:

To calculate the price including the standard rate of VAT (20%) multiply the price, excluding VAT, by 1.2.

To calculate the price including the reduced rate of VAT (5%) multiply the price, excluding VAT, by 1.05.

Price exclusive of VAT:

To calculate the price excluding the standard rate of VAT (20%) divide the price, including VAT, by 1.2.

To calculate the price excluding the reduced rate of VAT (5%) divide the price, including VAT, by 1.05

Set the record straight!

It is really important to keep good and clear records of the VAT you are paying and the VAT you are charging. I keep a separate summary account for my VAT which is a simple Excel spreadsheet where I record what I have charged out in VAT and what I have paid to others in VAT.

You will need to keep your VAT records for at least 6 years, in the event HMRC should ever wish to inspect them.

You can keep your records in various formats e.g. electronically, this could be an Excel spreadsheet or using online accounting software, e.g. Sage or Quickbooks or paper.

If you should lose a VAT invoice, then ask your supplier to let you have a duplicate and mark it as a duplicate.

As I mentioned earlier, you could also engage the services of an accountant to help you with your end of year Tax and VAT returns if you do not feel confident or comfortable with doing these yourself.

Points to consider

It is important to note that HMRC will make a charge if they should ever inspect your records and they feel they are not in order.

HMRC will charge a penalty fee for not submitting VAT returns on time – they do not accept any excuses!

4. **Do you want to register yourself and complete your own VAT returns or would you prefer to engage the services of a qualified and experienced accountant?**

   You do not have to deal with your own VAT returns if you feel 'uncomfortable' with this, you can ask a qualified accountant to do this for you. An accountant will charge you for handling your VAT returns and your end of year Tax return, so shop around to find out what your local accountants will charge if you would prefer this option.

5. **Are there different VAT rules when working with International Clients?**

   Being virtual assistants means we can work anywhere in the world and so it is not uncommon to work with international clients. VAT has slightly different rules applied when working with international clients and this can be quite complicated, it depends on your 'place of supply of services' and personal circumstances (e.g. where your client is based, EU/USA. It is not possible for me to add all the information on this subject to this book, but you can find more information by following this link and apply it to the way you work.

https://www.gov.uk/guidance/vat-how-to-work-out-your-place-of-supply-of-services

6. **Seeking professional advice**

I am sure you have now realised that VAT can be quite complicated. I would always recommend that you speak with an accountant before you register your business for VAT to ensure that your decision is an informed one and that you are fully aware of all the facts and implications of VAT registration, if you feel unsure in any way.

PART 3 – MARKETING

Who could be the clients of a Virtual Assistant?

The clients that virtual assistants work for come from a wide range of business sectors. Below is a list of the most common ones and while it's not a definitive list, it will help you to get an idea:

- Sole Traders
- Small to Medium Enterprises (SMEs)
- Micro Businesses
- Coaches and Trainers
- Medical Professionals
- Tradesmen
- Business Consultants
- Entrepreneurs
- Charitable and Third Sector Organisations
- Busy Executives
- Legal Professionals
- Authors
- Property management

Understanding where your clients are likely to come from (which will be based on your skills, knowledge and experience) is half the battle when the time comes to begin your marketing. Each business sector will need to be communicated with in a certain way; for example, the marketing message you send to a charity may be different to that of small-sized business.

Business Statistics

Below are some very interesting statistics based on the number of businesses in the UK, which will help to illustrate why virtual assistants are becoming more sought after and why small business owners are on the look-out for affordable and reliable business support to help them develop their own companies.

Statistics provided courtesy of the "House of Commons Library – Business Statistics – Briefing Paper Number SN06152 – December 2017"

This note presents a statistical analysis of businesses in the UK.

It includes information on the number of businesses since 2000, small businesses, business by region, businesses by industry, business births and deaths and information on female representation in business.

- In 2017, there were 5.7 million businesses in the UK.
- Over 99% of businesses are Small or Medium Sized businesses – employing 0-249 people
- 5 million (96%) businesses were micro-businesses – employing 0-9 people. Micro-businesses accounted for 33% of employment and 22% of turnover.
- In London, there were 1,519 businesses per 10,000 resident adults. In the North East there were 657 per 10,000 resident adults.
- The service industries accounted for 74% of businesses, 79% of employment and 71% of turnover.
- The manufacturing sector accounted for 5% of businesses, 10% of employment and 15% of turnover.
- There were 414,000 business births and 328,000 business deaths in 2015.

Business Networking – What's It All About?

Networking events are a great way to meet other business-mined people, build professional relationships and, as part of that process, develop your client base.

Remember, you are now self-employed and so you are responsible for finding your own work. These events are a good way for you to make connections and introduce yourself and your services to others. **Never** *use these events for direct selling* however. They're all about building relationships with other businesses and, over time, work will start to come your way once people get to know more about you and what you do.

Networking has a language all of its own and comes in different forms:

- Speed networking
- Formal networking
- Relaxed networking
- Forums and business clubs
- Social networking

Let's take a look at each one to give you an idea of the different types of networking available to you and how they usually work. Again, this is not an exhaustive list but it will give you a good steer on which format may be the most likely to work for you. I suggest you try them all to find out which ones are likely to be of benefit to you.

Familiarise yourself with the different options and how each format operates.

Speed Networking

This usually involves sitting around a table while facing another business person. You have around two minutes to introduce yourself and your company to them, and once your two minutes are up, the person opposite you will have two minutes to introduce themselves and their company to you. When you have both had two minutes, you will then move down a seat and you repeat this process. This continues until you have spoken with everyone around the table. This is a good way to 'quickly' introduce yourself to other businesses. However, it is more difficult for people to remember everyone they have spoken with in such a short period of time and to build professional relationships with this form of networking.

Formal Networking

Formal networking events tend to follow a set structure and have a certain way of operating. Delegates and visitors alike will be expected to follow that structure, which is likely to run a little like this:

- Meet for coffee, register and open networking

- A one/two minute opportunity for each attendee to deliver their 'elevator pitch' to the room (more on this later).

- A guest speaker or selected member will then be invited to deliver a ten minute (sometimes it can be longer) spotlight presentation on a topic. It tends to be related to their business, but it's not necessarily a sales pitch (you could volunteer to give presentations at networking events if you were so minded).

- One to one conversations with two or three other attendees. After you've listened to the elevator pitches of each of the attendees, you may be asked to choose three who you think will make for a good connection or someone who you feel may be able to help. You're able to arrange a one to one meeting with them for around 10 minutes – effectively five minutes for you and five for them.

- You may be asked to take one of your business contacts along with you to each meeting.

- You may have to commit to attending all the meetings.

- There will be a charge and some are expensive. You may have to pay a joining fee and then pay for your food on arrival at each meeting.

The more formal and structured networking groups include BNI and 4N.

More Relaxed Networking

This form of networking comes in many guises. It could take the form of an evening meal where you'll sit at one of a number of tables and introduce yourself to the others sat there. Equally, it could be an open networking event where you'll eat, chat and listen to guest speakers. The format really depends on whoever is organising and running the event, but they will usually tell you what the format is, in advance. If not, ask them, if you feel you would rather know before going along.

Networking is about making connections and raising awareness of who you are and what you do. It should never be used for the 'hard sell'. Trying that tactic usually results in people finding an excuse to get away from you. Start a conversation with someone in the room by introducing yourself, finding out their name and asking what they do. This will break the ice and strike up a conversation where you can get to know them and their business a little more. When they have told you about themselves, they would then usually ask about you and what you do.

Food is often provided at networking events but there is a cost element to this so check if you are expected to contribute. Most will offer your first visit free of charge to give you an opportunity to try the meeting and see if it works for you

Networking events are usually held early in the morning, at lunchtimes or evenings and the times vary.

As I mentioned above, networking can be expensive and so try a few different ones and see what works for you before signing up and paying long-term membership fees.

If you hear the term 'open networking' this simply means that you can wander around the meeting room and talk to people, find out who they are and what services they offer. Again, it's all about building those professional relationships I mentioned earlier.

Before attending the meeting you will need to prepare what is called your 'elevator pitch'. This is simply your one/two minute introduction (the time differs from group to group depending on their format) so you'll need to include your name, your company name and some information about *how you can help people and solve their professional problems.* Telling a brief story (while remembering your time limit) of how you successfully helped one of your clients (or someone you worked with) can work well as it demonstrates how you could potentially help those in the room. Practice your elevator pitch regularly as you will need to deliver it at most networking events. Delivered well, it will give the attendees something to think about - how they or someone they know may be able to use the services you are offering.

You can include business tips in your elevator pitch; something that will lead them to think of you as someone who is both helpful and really knows their stuff. Sure, standing up and presenting your elevator pitch in front of a crowd of unknown people can seem a bit daunting at first, but you'll find that you get used to it over time and the more you get to know the attendees the more relaxed you will feel. It's the same for everyone, so you are not alone!

Forums and Business Club Networking

Forums and business clubs are essentially networking coupled with business coaching and learning. These will often feature guest speakers who will speak on a variety of topics and offer business coaching and training courses – some free – and so it is well worth checking out what is available in your area and signing up to attend. You can also learn a lot by attending groups like this while building up a good list of contacts at the same time.

Social networking

You never really know where that next potential client may come from, someone you meet at a wedding or birthday party, a local event you may be attending, I met one of my clients at Church! Always be prepared, keep some business cards with you, just in case!

Tips

- Always aim to arrive at the networking event when it begins. When I first started out, I personally found it easier to start a conversation with someone who may also have just entered the room, or the next person that appeared after me, if I was the first to arrive. I felt more comfortable with this arrangement, rather than arriving when the event had already started to find numerous people already speaking to each other and having to find a way to join in.

- If there are two people standing face to face, they might be in the middle of a business transaction, so you should not attempt to join in.

- If you are wearing a jacket, unfasten it after arriving. You'll come across less stuffy and more relaxed and approachable.

- Without going over the top, wear or carry something that stands out. People often remember quirky items, such as a certain necklace or a memorable notebook. If they see them regularly they then start to associate you with that item, so choose wisely.

- If you see a group of people speaking to each other, it's okay to join in! To do this all you have to do is ask if you can join them. If you join in you may want to simply listen at first, as this will help you to get a good idea of what they are talking about and the manner in which they go about it.

- Remember to take plenty of business cards with you to all networking events, so that people you talk to can follow up on your conversation and make contact.

- When you are handed a business card from other people in the room, it is always a good idea to write on the back the name of the person you spoke with (if this is different to the name on the card), the date of the event, which event it was and perhaps which service they offered that interested you most. This serves as a good reminder as to who they are and where you met them should they get in touch or you need to contact them at some future point in time. Add these details to your contact database for contact purposes.

- Networking events are also a great way to seek advice from other professionals. Advice is often freely shared as it gives attendees at the meetings an opportunity to showcase their industry knowledge and, who knows, they may know someone who would benefit from working with you. Offer to meet them at some point in the near future for a coffee and a chat as a way of following up.

- As well as networking with the people in the room, always remember that you are effectively networking with the businesses they know and can refer you to.

- Networking events are great for finding other professionals who may be of help to one of your own clients. This makes your services even more valuable and attractive. My clients often benefit from my business connections.

- When you find some events you like, diarise them so that you don't miss out and can plan your work around each one where possible.

- Think about having a stand at a networking or other event (do not pay a lot for this). This gives you an opportunity to perhaps show samples of your work, put some of your printed marketing material on display, answer questions, showcase a list of your services and raise your profile.

- Be clear about your objectives. Who are you looking to connect with? What size and type of businesses are you looking to provide assistance to? When delivering your pitch, specifically mention these factors so that people in the room know what you are looking for. As I mentioned above, you are also networking with other businesses that *they* know.

- You may be invited by someone you meet at a networking event to meet for a coffee. This may be because they are trying to persuade you to sign up to their networking group for long term, it may be that they would like to try help you make connections, they may feel that you would be a good connection for them. There could be many reasons **BUT** regardless of the reasons I would always recommend you let someone know where you are going and meet in a very public place. Perhaps ask a family member or friend to send you a text message when you are at the meeting to check all is okay. **Think very carefully about your personal safety**.

You attend networking events to make business contacts, but remember, it can be expensive. So be sure to make good use of your time and not spend too much of it in general chit chat. Try to 'work the room'; speak to as many people as possible, but ensure that you don't come across as being rude by rushing around from delegate to delegate. Say hello to the ones you have met before to keep the relationship building process going, but make a point of speaking to people you have not met before and spend most of your time on this to further build your network of contacts.

Even when you're very busy, you should always make time to go networking, otherwise your connections can start to go cold. Try not to 'dilute' your networking time by trying to attend too many events; go to some regularly but don't overdo it. Do enough to build professional relationships as, after all, networking is all about developing the 'know, like and trust' cycle. The more people get to know you, the more they get to like you and the more they like you, the more likely it will be that they will refer you to their own clients or other contacts.

Don't be afraid to tell people that you are new to networking. More seasoned networkers will be only too happy to help you. You should also find that the organisers of the event will introduce you to people who can help you along.

PRACTICAL TASK #10

Have a search on Google for the following:

http://www.bni.co.uk/
www.4networking.biz
https://www.eventbrite.co.uk
http://www.britishchambers.org.uk/find-your-chamber/
http://www.ebusinessclub.biz/

See what they offer and sign up to attend at least two events. Remember not to commit yourself to anything longer-term at this stage until you have gone along and assessed whether or not they will work for you. Try to attend at least one networking meeting per week to begin with and see how you get on from there.

Creating your 'Elevator Pitch'

Let's start at the beginning…why is it called an 'elevator pitch' I hear you ask. The term 'elevator pitch' is slang and it basically means a short speech that describes a service, product or idea, it is said, should usually take around 60 seconds to deliver your short speech - the same time it takes you to take a short elevator ride – hence the name 'elevator pitch'.

Your elevator pitch will be essential when attending networking events, this is your opportunity to tell people in the room who you are and what you do. You have around 1 to 2 minutes (depending on the networking event you go to) to make people remember you and so make full use of that time!

Let's take a look at how you can create your own elevator pitch and how it may come in useful…

You have just bumped into a former colleague at a networking event and, after some general chit chat, he asks you "So what does your new company do then?" You stand there with your mouth wide open and then....silence. Where on earth do you actually start?

Well, while you tried to get your thoughts together, your former colleague had to leave to get to another appointment. Chances are had you been better prepared he would have stuck around long enough for you to arrange a meeting with him.

This is one example of when having an 'elevator pitch' would certainly have made better use of the time you had with your former colleague.

Creating your Pitch

It will take you a while to create your pitch and get it right. It's highly likely you will create several versions before finding the one you feel happy with. You may want to create a few different ones to use for different purposes and in different situations, for example, you may want to use one to promote your services and one to promote a new product you are introducing – varying your approach will keep people interested in what you have to say. You want it to sound natural when spoken in front of an audience.

Technique

An elevator pitch is a short speech that you use to spark interest in what you do. You can also use them to create an interest in you personally – this might be a particular project you are working on or a new service you have introduced.

Your elevator pitch should be interesting, memorable and succinct (to the point).

Describe What You Do

Start your speech by explaining what you do. Give an example of how you helped a recent client – how did you solve their problems? If possible, add a statistic to evidence the value of what you do and how you help people.

When to use an Elevator Pitch

Use your elevator pitch to introduce yourself and your services to potential clients, let people know about something new that you may be working on, if you have started a new initiative. You have a great idea…tell people about it!

1.   *Identifying your Aim*

The best place to begin creating your elevator pitch is to start by thinking about the objective of your pitch. You need to grab the attention of the audience immediately you begin to speak.

For example, do you want to tell potential clients about your company? Do you have a new service or idea you want to tell them about? Do you have some tips or information that you would like to share with other business owners?

When creating your pitch, **you** should be the first one to be excited and enthusiastic about it, if you are, then others will be. Your audience may not remember all what you have said, but they **will** remember your enthusiasm.

Ask yourself this question as you start writing: what do you want your audience to remember most about you?

Example:

Imagine you're creating an elevator pitch for a networking event that describes what you do. You could say, "My name is XXX and my company is XXX and I help people with their admin problems." But that's not very memorable is it!

A better explanation would be, "My company develops administrative strategies to help businesses to grow and develop. This results in a significant increase in efficiency and effectiveness for business owners."

This is much more interesting and shows the value you provide to business owners.

2   *What is your USP?*

Your elevator pitch needs to express your **Unique Selling Point** or USP.

What makes you, your company or your idea, unique? You can tell people what your USP is when you have talked about what you do.

Example:

To highlight what makes you unique, you could say something like this:

"We use a different approach to what we do because we like to actually visit each client to find out exactly what they need and how their systems and processes can be made more productive and efficient. Although this process takes a little more time, it means our clients are, on average, 98% happy with the services we provide."

Never say '100% happy...' because there is always room for improvement and nobody is that perfect!

3.   *Start with a Question*

To engage the attention of your audience immediately you speak, prepare an open-ended question (questions that can't be answered with a simple "yes" or "no") to involve them in the conversation.

Ensure you are able to answer any questions your audience may ask.

Example:

You may ask "So, how many of you know what a Virtual Assistant is" or "How many of you know how a Virtual Assistant helps businesses to grow and develop?"

4.   *Put it all Together*

When you've prepared each part of your pitch, you then need to put it all together.

Read your pitch to yourself and time how long it takes you to deliver it. It should not take more than 1 or 2 minutes. If it goes on for too long you may lose the interest of your audience, which is the last thing you want.

If necessary, cut out anything that does not need to be there. Remember, your pitch needs to be lively and compelling, so the shorter it is, the better!

Example:

Here's how your pitch could come together:

"Hi my name is XXX my company develops administrative strategies to help businesses to grow and develop. This results in a significant increase in efficiency and effectiveness for business owners.

We use a different approach to what we do because we like to actually visit each client to find out exactly what they need and how their systems and processes can be made more productive and efficient. Although this process takes a little more time, it means our clients are, on average, 99% happy with the services we provide."

So, how do you deal with all of the paperwork in your company?"

Towards the end, let people in the room know what or who you are looking for, is it a web developer for one of your clients? Are you looking to 'connect with small charitable organisations'? If people know what you are looking for, they may be able to help or introduce you to someone they know.

End your pitch with something like 'My name is [your name] from [your company name] thank you'.

5. *Practice*

Like most things, practice makes perfect. If you don't practice, it's likely you'll talk too fast, sound unnatural or forget what you were going to say.

Set aside some time in your diary to practice your pitch regularly. The more you practice, the more natural your pitch will become. You want your pitch to come across naturally - and not as a heavy sales speech.

Be mindful of your body language as you speak. Your body language transmits just as much information to the listener as your words do. Practice in front of a mirror or, if possible, in front of a colleague or friend until the pitch feels natural.

As you get used to delivering your pitch, it's fine to vary it to suit the occasion. The idea is to sound natural and not 'mechanical' or that it's been pre-prepared, even though it has been!

Don't be afraid to use a script to read from at networking events, if people know you are new to networking they will happily make allowances to help you.

Finding clients - various ways you can do this

This is probably one of the most difficult skills you will have to develop. Finding clients will take you out of your comfort zone, but it will also make you a more confident person, given time. As well as networking there are several other ways you can reach clients such as social media, leaflet drops, advertising, free listing directories, e-shots, your website, logo/branding, job sites, asking current clients if they know of anyone who may benefit from your services. Let's take a look at some options:

Social Media

Social media as a marketing tool is the norm, in fact I would go as far as to say it is 'expected' in the modern business world we live in as well as being a part of our everyday lives. It can be a minefield because there are so many different platforms to choose from: Twitter, Facebook, Google+ Blogger, LinkedIn, Pinterest....the list goes on. It's simply not possible for me to give you all the details of how social media works and how to use it in this book (that's a whole book in itself) but I will try to provide you with a little taster that will help you to make a start.

It is possible to gain work from social media but you need to first put in place a strategy as it can be very time consuming and draw you away from other important matters. Choose your platforms carefully and concentrate your efforts on those where your target clients hang out. Here are a few tips to get you started:

- Think of social media as being a form of networking online instead of in person.

- Social media is great for 'advertising' what you do by showcasing your skills and knowledge to others.

- Think about which platforms are the best to reach your target audience. I use Twitter, Facebook and LinkedIn:

  - **Twitter** is great for joining in a conversation and introducing new services or events

  - **Facebook** is great for pictures - and virtual assistant groups. There are some great groups for you to join and they are a good way of helping other virtual assistants by offering help and advice. It also gives you an opportunity to ask other virtual assistants questions.

  - **LinkedIn** is one of the best platforms to build business contacts.

- Choosing your platforms carefully will help you to focus on the ones that are more likely to bring reward.

- Some social media platforms are designed more for products than services, such as Pinterest or Facebook.

- When using social media, you need to have a strategy planned in advance. Focus on one topic and post about that topic on your different platforms for around a couple of weeks – but not every day! Then change to a different topic. 'Drip feed' your audience.

- Spend some time looking at what other people are posting about. This will give you a good idea of what sort of information is being shared, what's popular and how it's done.

- Post content that is relevant and informative or (professionally) humorous.

- Look at what your target market is up to: what are they posting about? Look for events they may be attending, what projects they're working on and if they run any groups you could potentially join. The more you know about your ideal client the easier it is to connect with them.

- A small proportion of your posts should be about you – about your skills and what you offer. This will help you to raise awareness of who you are, what you do and what you have to offer. It can put you foremost in the mind of potential clients.

- The greater proportion of your posts (around 80%) should be about how you help your clients, how you solve their problems and ease their business pains.

- Try to post at least two or three times per week, but be realistic. As you get busier with client work you may have to re-assess how much of your time is spent on social media. The client always comes first!

- Social media is a great way to raise your profile.

- Signing up to Twitter, Facebook and LinkedIn is free of charge.

- If someone should send you a request to link up with them on LinkedIn, send them a personal message and introduce yourself and the services you provide. Keep it brief and to the point and without sounding 'pushy' though. After all, they asked for you to connect with them and should not be surprised when you send them a message to introduce yourself.

- I would suggest keeping your social media platforms public, as you want people to find and connect with you and share your blog posts (more on blog posts below). Because you will be using different social media platforms to reach different audiences it is a good idea not to link them as each will have their own type of audience. Not everyone who reads your LinkedIn posts will want to see your Twitter posts.

- Always point your social media posts back to your website. Add your website URL to each post so that when people click on it, it takes them to the appropriate page of your website, which is where the relevant content and information will be. Don't put all the necessary details on your social media posts, send the reader to your website to discover the information they're searching for.

- When adding your photo to your social media account, upload one of yourself. Don't use an obscure picture as people like to know who they are connecting with and that they have the right person so, for example don't use a picture of your favourite pet. You will find on social media that there will likely be a number of people across the globe who share the same name as you.

- As soon as you can, arrange to have a professional head and shoulders photo taken of yourself by a photographer. This can be used on your social media platforms and website. It is easy to tell which are professionally taken photos from 'selfies' – and each photo affects how you're perceived.

- Social media is about building relationships. Interact with your contacts.

- The number of Likes on your Facebook and having 500 followers on Twitter mean very little if they are not your ideal client or someone of relevance to you or your business. Try to build good quality, rather than quantity, of contacts.

- Remember that social media is instant and so as soon as you post something it goes out across the network to everyone who is following you. Proofread your posts carefully before pressing the 'send' button! Many of the social media platforms offer an 'edit' feature and so if you do spot a mistake, you can always go back and correct it.

- You can schedule your posts via platforms such as Hootsuite. This enables you to schedule your posts so that they go out at certain times of the week across your social media platforms.
https://hootsuite.com.

- Think about the times at which your posts are going to go out. When are your followers most likely to be actively engaging with social media? If you post in the morning, they can read what you've written on their way to work; at lunchtimes they can read while having lunch; in the evenings on the way home or once they've got indoors.

- Although not strictly a social media platform, I would recommend you register with 'Google My Business'. You will need to open a Google account if you don't already have one, but it's free and it helps people to find you. You can find more information by using this link to open an account or register.
https://www.google.com/business/

PRACTICAL TASK #11

Open up an account on two social media platforms, perhaps LinkedIn and Facebook or Twitter.

https://twitter.com
https://www.linkedin.com
https://www.facebook.com

Join some virtual assistant forums on the different platforms and have a go at answering any questions that other virtual assistants may be asking. Post any questions you may have too.

Just a word of caution, many people who run groups on Facebook have what are known as 'House Rules', these set down the rules that you have to use if you are posting to their group. Many do not like you to post links to your blogs and website and to ask for 'likes' on your Facebook page. If you join any Facebook groups, ensure you read the house rules as to what is or is not permitted.

When you have opened your social media accounts, link up with five people. Introduce yourself to the various groups you have joined, tell them briefly about yourself and what services you are providing, but avoid doing so in a sales-type fashion.

Spend some time looking at what other people are posting about. This will give you a good idea of what sort of information you can post and how to go about it.

Blogging

Another form of social media is 'blogging' on your own website, speak to your web developer about this or add a blog or latest news page if you are building your own website.

A blog is just a piece of information, it could be a new service you have introduced or tips for making something easier or faster, it could be some new rules or regulations that are coming into force that may affect your ideal client. When you post a blog on your website, you can use your own social media platforms to post people back to it. This is how you 'drive' traffic to your website.

Some social media platforms do not like long web links (URLs) and so they may need to be shorted and to do this you can use Googles own URL shortener. This is easy to use and when you have shorted your web link you can copy and paste this into your Twitter post. This could, of course, be the link to your own website blog/latest news page. As social media platforms, such as Twitter, limit you to how many characters you can use in a blog post, using a URL shortener is essential! Just copy and paste the URL you would like to shorten.
https://goo.gl/

As well as blogging on your own website you can also write blog posts for others as a 'guest blogger'. This gives you an opportunity to showcase your knowledge to a wider audience. You can also add a little piece about yourself and also add your weblink in the process. Do not make this into a 'sales pitch'. Remember it is not about you, it is about your audience and what they want to read or learn about. They can get further information about you and your services from your website.

Take a look for websites that blog and serve your ideal client, but not that of a direct competitor. Make an approach to the owner of the website and make your approach personal. Why have you chosen them? What can you offer to their audience? It's likely that they may ask for samples of posts you've written, so have a few prepared just in case.

You could also post on your social media platforms (not on competitor groups though) and ask if anyone is on the lookout for guest bloggers to write about specific topics.

Remember to link all of your blog posts back to your website. It's no good having a good, professional-looking website if no-one knows you exist or how to find you.

It is essential to add social media buttons/plug-ins to your blog posts wherever possible. This enables other people to share your posts, taking you to a far wider audience.

Try to post a blog at least two to three times a week. You'll get 'rewarded' by Google for refreshing your website content in the process. Take a look at 'Hub Spot' for some ideas on what you could start blogging about.
http://blog.hubspot.com/

To blog or not to blog – that is the question!

Whether to blog or not is usually a hot topic on social media and at networking events. Some people are not sure if they need a blog, some people do not know what to write about even if they do have a blog and some people just think it a waste of time and only useful for helping people to find you and your website.

There is no easy, quick or simple answer to whether blogs are important and whether you should have one (I wish there was!) but it really depends on what you are looking for from a blog!

Should I write a blog?

You should write a blog if you want:

- people to know about you, what you do and how you can help
- your website to be found amongst the billions of other sites that are out there

- to showcase your skills and expertise to potential clients
- to share your own posts with others
- establish yourself as a 'go to' person for the services you provide
- share your client case studies and testimonials with others
- raise your own profile within the virtual assistant industry
- need help and support from others
- build your own network of contacts
- to offer blog writing or editing as a service to clients

You should not write a blog if you:

- struggle with good grammar and spelling
- you have enough work without needing to blog to find more work
- don't know what to say or what audience you are trying to connect with
- you can't spare the time
- you feel it irrelevant to you and what you are trying to achieve as a business owner

Writing a blog

If you do decide that writing blogs is for you, then what you are looking for, ultimately, is for someone to engage your services! You need to put yourself in the minds of your potential and ideal clients. So, think about the person you are trying to reach, are they a builder, medical professional, author, electrician, not for profit organisation? What would they find interesting, what would <u>they</u> want to read about. You could research the internet and find groups or organisations who offer updates. For example, if your ideal client was a not for profit organisation, then it would be worth you signing up to the Charity Commission newsletters, you could then blog about any news or information that you may feel relevant. Yes, it is likely that most charities will already be receiving these newsletters but......some do not have time to read all of the posts and newsletters and so do not assume your ideal client will know about any important changes or updates that may be on the horizon. Potential clients will not be aware of you and how you can help and so you need to let them know.

So what should I write about?

There are several things you could write about and that would draw the attention of potential and ideal clients and here are a few examples to get you started:

Hints and tips

These are the things that matter to your potential client. So it could be something like '5 new challenges introduced by the Charity Commissioners', '5 things you can do to in your coffee break', '5 new systems/apps to improve the way you work'.

By writing blog posts about what matters to your ideal clients you are showing that you know what you are talking about, up to date on what is happening in 'their world' and what affects them and their business. It also shows that you have the industry knowledge that will benefit them.

'How to....'

These types of blog seem to do quite well on social media. These are known as 'tutorial posts'. These can be in written form or as videos on Facebook or YouTube – pictures and videos – something visual - are really good to use on social media. These posts are a great way to showcase your skills, knowledge and experience.

Think about some of the questions your clients, or perhaps people you worked with in the past, have asked you. How did you solve their particular problem, that they just couldn't solve themselves. Create a 'how to' video that will help others solve that same problem.

Keep any videos short, as business owners have a very limited attention span due to pressure of work – 5 mins maximum. You do not need to give all of your 'secrets' away, just enough to let people know that you know your industry and can solve a problem.

For example, I wrote a blog on 'How To' get rid of that annoying black line that appears in Word documents when you press the return key (it puts a black line along the whole page and you just couldn't delete it). Some of my clients had asked me how to resolve this problem. It took me all of two minutes to do this for them. I did offer to write this down for one of my clients – feeling perhaps I was doing myself out of a job! – but he replied saying "I have not got time to sort out those sort of things and anyway, I have you to do it for me and you can deal with it much better and faster than I can". Most clients do not have time, or the inclination, to deal with these kind of tasks themselves. I need not have worried!

Case studies and testimonials

I have used many case studies in blogs to demonstrate to people how I can help them. This gives readers an idea of:

- what type of client I was helping
- what action and steps I took to resolve some of the problems clients were facing
- what systems I introduced to make clients more productive and efficient
- what challenges clients were facing and how I helped them to meet and win those challenges
- what impact my help and support had on the client and their business – the results of my input.

- what potential clients, who are reading my posts and facing the same problems and challenges, can expect when working with me.
- how my skills, experience and knowledge can help them to grow and develop their own business.

When posting case studies or testimonials on blogs or on your website you do not necessarily have to mention the client's name, but doing so gives it validity. I always ask my client, as a matter of courtesy, if it is okay for me to post their testimonial on my social media platforms or on my website, when including their name.

Client Interview

Client interviews are a great way to let your clients 'do the talking' for you. These can be done by Skype or a short video of them speaking about how you have helped them and how they have benefitted from working with you.

How do I write a blog post?

As I mentioned earlier in this book, social media could be covered in a book all on its own! There are loads of platforms to use and different ways you can use those platforms. There are even some websites that are dedicated purely to blog post writing.

That said, some basic advice I would offer is

- Don't spend too much time thinking or worrying about it.

- Keep it clear and easy to read.

- Keep it succinct – to the point!

- When writing your post, decide who it is for, why are you writing it, what is the post about?

- Have a basic strategy – e.g. post about the same topic for a couple of weeks, but different areas of that topic. Take your readers on a short 'journey' with you.

- Diarise when to post your blogs – this will help you to keep them up to date.

- Try to write your blogs in advance.

- You could use a plug-in to schedule your blog posts, such as Hootsuite.

- Don't post straight away, write it and then come back to it later, to ensure you are happy with it and that there are no spelling or grammar mistakes.

- End your post with a call to action – what do you want the person reading the post to do when they have read it? Call you? Sign up for one of your webinars? Download a free tips booklet you have written?

- Look at other virtual assistant websites to see what they write about and how they write, it may give you some inspiration!

- Use hashtags in your post wherever possible to help people find it e.g #VirtualAssistant (notice that there is no space in-between virtual and assistant) #freelancer – if people are searching on Twitter, LinkedIn or Facebook for, example, posts that contain 'virtual assistant' or 'freelancer' - by putting the hashtag in front of the words will bring up your post for them to read.

Leaflets

Believe it or not, there is a strategy to leaflets. I undertook some research of small business owners and asked them what they thought about leaflets and this is what I found:

- They preferred to see the benefits to them stated on the leaflet. They felt that too many people focus on the services they are providing and not what they can do to help a business.

- They liked the idea of using both sides of the leaflet. One side with contact details and one side with the benefits to them.

- They liked images to make the leaflet more interesting.

- They get many leaflets and tend to read the ones that stand out from the crowd.

- They did not like too many colours as this made reading a little 'over powering'.

- They did not particularly like leaflets made from cheap paper as this gives the impression the services offered would be 'cheap' and 'cheerful'.

- They preferred bullet points to long winded paragraphs due to the short time they have to read them.

Deliver a few first to test the water. If you do not receive any response, then try changing the images and tweak your text.

Leaflets take time, you may not receive any work or enquiries from them immediately, but they will help to 'sow the seed'. Some business owners may put your leaflet in a draw in the event they may need it later.

You could put your leaflets in an envelope addressed to the business owner, this is a little more time consuming, but may bring rewards.

Try to be methodical with your leaflet drop, think about who you are trying to reach and where they would be. I would suggest you do not use the 'scatter gun' approach.

When you find the right formula that works for you, then try delivering your leaflets over a wider area.

Advertising

When I first started out I tried various ways of advertising - magazines, local newspapers etc - but this brought very little return in terms of clients. However, advertising in this way can serve to get your name out there. I wouldn't recommend spending lots of money on large advertisements or advertising in magazines/newspapers in general, it's much better and more effective to have small but regular adverts in local, cheaper, magazines. Advertising is all about seeing your brand everywhere, which is why I mentioned earlier in this book the importance of having a social media presence. Everyone knows McDonalds, don't they? If you were to ask someone what colour the letter 'M' for McDonalds is, they would immediately say yellow as they're used to seeing it all the time. The same principle applies to you and your brand – the more people see it, the more they'll remember it. Advertising does not mean you need to spend a lot of money!

You could even use your car to advertise with. How often do you go to the supermarket, networking events, days out, or visit your clients and park in their car park alongside all *their* clients? Your car goes wherever you go. Consider having your logo, email address and a brief statement or slogan in the back window of your car. I say back window because those following you on the road can see the back of your car but are unable to see the doors! The same applies to parking; if you are parked next to someone, other people cannot see the sides of your car, but they can see the back of your car as they walk past. This is a very cost-effective and affordable way to advertise your brand. Search on Google for marketing/sign design companies in your local area that would be able to design/print/attach a transfer(s) to your vehicle for you and likely costs.

Free Listing Directories

When I first started I placed free entries in the Yellow Pages, Thomson Local and Scoot as these offer online listings alongside the traditional paper versions. However, please be aware that you may receive lots of time-consuming sales calls which are unlikely to result in any work. Instead, I recommend that you register with directories that are specifically geared towards virtual assistants and use your resources for networking, which will bring greater reward in the long-run.

E-Shots

Simply put, an e-shot is an electronic leaflet/newsletter sent by email, usually sent using software such as Mailchimp and Mad Mimi.

I personally enjoy using Mailchimp for my e-shots. It's really easy to use and enables you to add images, links to your website and your social media platforms too. You can send e-shots to just under 2,000 subscribers free of charge. This is a great way to tell your subscribers about a new service you're launching, an event you may be organising or to simply share hints and tips. It has all kinds of uses and it takes only a little time to put together if you prepare a template and update it as and when you send out your information.

With e-shots I always aim to provide good, useful content. Something that the reader can take away with them, such as a 'hot tip' or a 'how to do' something. These always seem to provoke a positive response. When preparing your content, focus on how you can help people.

Only send out quality information on an occasional basis., for example, if you would like to send a newsletter to your contacts, only send one once a month. Do not spam (sending lots of irrelevant information to a large number of people for advertising purposes) as this will make you very unpopular very quickly. Email addresses entered into, for example, Mailchimp or Mad MiMi, need to come from your contacts who have given you explicit permission to market to them. There are strict operational codes that forbid spamming when using these types of software. Remember, under GDPR you need explicit permission to market to people.

When creating your newsletter, think carefully about the content you intend to add, including any images. Always include your logo, website address and a call to action message. You could also include a suitable, professional image of yourself. Diarise when you intend to send out your e-shot and be consistent. Keep your e-shots fresh, simple and easy to read and try not to overuse the same images.

Mailchimp operates by utilising 'lists'. These lists are basically your contact emails, the people you will be sending your e-shot to. You may need different lists for different purposes as the messages you send will likely target different audiences and business sectors. Think about who you are sending your e-shot to and what category they fall into, e.g. your clients, small business owners, charities and so forth.

Mailchimp also provides useful stats and informs you as to who has or hasn't opened your e-shot. Just a word of caution however: from personal experience I can say that many e-shots are simply deleted and never read. Companies receive lots of them every day and don't have time to read them all in their entirety so remember that you will be competing for their attention. Therefore, make your e-shot stand out. Think of a good title or subject heading - something that will offer an incentive for the recipient to open and read it.

PRACTICAL TASK #12

Take a look at and MailChimp and Mad MiMi and open an account with one or each. Have a go at creating a template and adding images, your website address and social media links. It's great fun and helps you to focus on your business message, style and tone of voice. You can send a 'test' newsletter to yourself so that you can see what your newsletter will look like when your recipient receives it. This gives you an opportunity to check that all the links are working, the images look crisp and clear and that your spelling and grammar are all okay prior to sending to your marketing 'list'.
https://mailchimp.com
https://madmimi.com/

Testimonials

When people put together a marketing plan they often forget to add testimonials to the list. Testimonials are a great form of marketing. They add value and credence to your business and you as a person. They describe how you have helped clients which in turn gives other business owners a good idea of how they may benefit from working with you.

After a period of about six months or so, ask your client if they would help you by providing a testimonial of how they have benefitted from your services. This testimonial could be shared on your website, as a YouTube video, on your social media platforms or in your e-shots. A period of six months will enable your client to really understand how they have benefitted from your help and provide an honest appraisal. I have never had a client who has refused to give me a testimonial when I have approached them. Some clients have even offered to write one for me without me having to ask!

Clients generally appreciate your help and like to help in return if they can.

If they are on LinkedIn, ask if they could write a recommendation for you. These cannot be edited by you, which gives more weight to the content.

Don't hide testimonials away, they show people how good you are. Let everyone know about them! Remember that you have worked hard to earn that testimonial so show it off and be proud of your achievements.

Job Agencies

To be honest, I'm not a big fan of job agencies where being a VA is concerned, primarily because, in my experience, you cannot earn much money with them, they tend to offer very low rates, whereas I prefer to get paid what I am worth. You've taken many years to learn what you have learnt, attended many training sessions, worked hard on exam papers, self-taught yourself to enhance your skills – why then should you sell all of that knowledge and experience cheaply? When you are first starting out you may want to take on a little work from a job agency to help you out in terms of finding out what clients are looking for and helping pay some of the bills and expenses while you are setting up and building your own client base, but getting your own clients offers you the opportunity to charge higher rates, build your business and have a better lifestyle. If you feel working via an agency is for you, I do know some virtual assistants who use/have used People Per Hour.
https://www.peopleperhour.com

Your Website and Logo/Branding

As with many features of your business, try to avoid short-term solutions as these are often a false economy. Choose systems that will grow with you. Your website is no exception.

Believe me, you really will be judged by your website! Think of it as a shop window where you showcase your services, your credibility, your image and your brand. Having a good-looking website *really is* important. If it's poor it suggests that your service is poor too and it can have a detrimental effect on how you are perceived.

Plan your website carefully. I have set out below the main content you should look to include. You don't have to add everything straight away, but if you can then you'll find it to be an advantage.

Home Page – (also known as the landing page). This is the first page your visitors arrive at if they have typed your domain name into their search engine.

About – This is where you can tell your visitors about yourself, what experience you have and a little bit about you as a person.

Services – The services you have on offer to potential clients. Remember that this is your opportunity to showcase your skills and highlight your niche, if you've established what that is yet. Remember to point out how you can help clients to solve their 'pains'.

Blog – This is where you can share useful news and information with your website visitors.

Rates – Not all virtual assistants display their rates on their website. I personally like to be transparent and so prefer to advertise my rates, where this is possible. You can show rates per hour, per day, package prices and retainer costs. Displaying rates on your website does not mean that they are none-negotiable. The only person who can really make the decision on whether to display charges is you, because only you know how you want to work.

Contact - Provide your address, telephone number and a contact form as appropriate so that people get in touch should they have any queries or wish to request a quote.

<u>Newsletter sign-up</u> – Here you can capture data such as names and email addresses, but you need to think about incentives to get people to provide you with that information, such as signing up for a short e-book, a training course or a free webinar. Remember that with the GDPR you will need to make it clear what they are signing up to – just saying 'newsletter' does not really tell people what that actually means or includes.

<u>Testimonials/Case Studies</u> – These provide evidence and proof of your service standards and also give potential clients an idea of the kind of services you provide.

<u>Share buttons</u> – These allow people to share your blog posts across all forms of social media platforms.

<u>Privacy Policy</u>

As mentioned earlier in this guide under GDPR, this states your policy for the collection, storage and use of the visitors personal data. This document is intended for use on a website which collects:

- Basic, non-sensitive personal data (such as name, contact details) for the purpose of supplying services and;

- Information about the visitor's online behaviour and Cookies.

<u>General</u>

Draw a plan of how you would like your website to look. Think about how each page will link to another and the journey that you would like visitors to take as they browse the site. What colours would you like to use? What type of imagery would you prefer? Try to keep your website easy to navigate, uncluttered and clean.

When you are happy with your website plan, you can then begin to work on your content.

Add a call to action on each page. Don't assume people will know what to do. Spell it out for them. Let the visitor to your site know what you want them to do – e.g. 'Call now for a no-obligation chat about how I can help you.'

If I am making amendments to my website I would usually ask someone to check it for me.

Most importantly of all, keep it up to date!

Think about the keywords you are going to use. These are the words or phrases that people will type into Google when they're trying to find services or products. Add these keywords into your website content.

SEO (Search Engine Optimisation) is what helps drive your website towards the first page on Google. When you post a blog on your website, Google 'rewards' you for it provided it has been well-written, structured and contains appropriate keywords.

PRACTICAL TASK #14

If you do not have the confidence or time to create a WordPress website yourself (or if you want an alternative platform), search on the internet to find website developers. Search for someone who deals with small businesses and is reputable. You'll need a website that looks professional, is mobile-responsive (meaning it looks and operates just as well when viewed on mobiles phones and tablets as it would on a laptop or PC), you have access to the site so that you are able to manage and edit the content yourself, you can add your social media links, a blog page with share buttons and can add testimonials too. These features will improve your marketing, professional appearance to potential clients and Google rankings. However, there will be a cost element to this standard of website and so you may like to look at adding some features at a later date to spread out the costs.

For those reading this book who are unfamiliar with WordPress, this is a free content management system that can be used to create your own website and blog content. WordPress is reportedly the most popular website management system on the web. You can find more information here:
https://wordpress.com

Domain Name

Your website address is your domain name.

Don't search for your domain name to check if it's in use until you are ready to create and launch your site. Domain registration companies buy domain names in bulk and if they see yours is already being searched for they may buy it themselves and then try to sell it to you at a much-inflated price.

Keep your domain name simple, memorable and easy to spell. Consider if you'd like to use your name or something that is related to what you do.

Think about whether you want a co.uk or a .com extension. I personally bought both. The co.uk cost £10 for two years and the .com cost me £15 for one year. There are a number of domain providers and one of the more popular ones is 123reg (and this is their domain name):
https://www.123-reg.co.uk

Hosting

If you decide to build your own website, it will need to be hosted – stored on a server owned by a hosting company. You don't necessarily need to have your hosting and website provided by the same company.

If you prefer to ask a web developer to build your website for you, ask them what their hosting charges are and what this charge includes, e.g does it include any support, does it include you having access to amend your own content as and when you wish and upload your own photos.

You don't need to purchase hosting just yet – do this when you are ready to go live with your website.

If you are going to buy your own domain name, you will need to give this to your web developer when he creates your website.

If your web developer is going to deal with your domain name for you, ensure it is registered in your own name and address so that you keep control of it.

Email address

Remember, you are setting yourself up as a professional business and you want to be perceived as such. I recommend you stay clear of using email addresses with suffixes such as Yahoo, Hotmail and so forth once you begin to work with clients.

You may have noticed I didn't include Gmail in the list above? This is because Google run a suite of online software that enables you to have a personalised business email address, online working calendars, online data storage and more. Google G Suite costs around £3.30 per user per month, which is a small amount for a big package. This can be accessed from your laptop, PC, phone and tablet, making you fully mobile. You will need to have your domain name set up ready to register with G Suite and you'll be provided with easy to follow step by step instructions to create your account. **https://gsuite.google.com**

I use Office 365 and this facilitates a business email address which I can use across all of my devices.

When sending or receiving emails I use an email signature. It looks professional and also acts as a 'disclaimer' with regard to any content that you send out while also providing brief contact information for you and your company – another good way to help build your name, reputation and brand!

If you have never created an email signature here is how to do this (using Microsoft Office 365 desktop):

Creating your Email Signature Message

Your email signature should be placed at the bottom of your emails – you can set this to add it automatically to emails you send or reply to. This gives your emails a very professional look and it is another form of brand building and advertising. Best of all, it's free!

1. Log into to your Office 365 account

2. Ensure you are on 'Outlook'

3. At the top left hand side of your toolbar, select the 'File' tab

4. Click on 'Options'

5. Select 'Mail' from the list on the left hand side

6. Click on 'Create or modify signatures for messages'

7. This will open up a dialogue box.

    At the top of this box you will see a small white box with the wording 'Automatically include my signature on new messages I compose' next to it – ensure this box is selected. This will automatically add your email signature to all the new emails you compose.

    Underneath this, you will see a second small white box with the wording 'Automatically include my signature on messages I forward or reply to' next to it – ensure this box is also selected. This will automatically add your email signature to all the emails you either respond to or forward to someone else.

8. In the large white box is where you can create your email signature. To give you an idea how one should look, I have set out below an example which may give you a little inspiration when creating yours:

———————

Erica Holden
Executive Virtual Assistant
Tel: [put your telephone number here]
www. [put your own web address here]

[Put your logo here – if you have one]

Help the environment, please do not print this email unless you really need to. Thank you.

This e-mail and any files transmitted with it are confidential, may be legally privileged and are for the sole use of the intended recipient. If you are not the intended recipient of this e-mail or any part of it please telephone us immediately on **[put your telephone number here]** or notify me by email at **[put your email address here]**. You should not use or disclose to any other person the contents of this e-mail or its attachments (if any), nor take copies.

I have taken every reasonable precaution to ensure that any attachment to this e-mail has been swept for viruses, but I cannot accept any liability for any loss or damage sustained as a result of software viruses and would advise that you carry out your own virus checks before opening any attachment. Please also note that e-mails may be falsified: in circumstances where the content of this e-mail is important you should not rely on its integrity without checking it by telephone.

———————

When you have created your email signature, test it by creating a 'New Email' to check it all looks okay.

<u>Logo/Branding</u>

Logos are a crucial feature of business marketing. Your logo is your company's main graphical representation to the world. It anchors your brand and it becomes the single most visible sign of what your company stands for and represents. A well-designed logo is an essential part of your marketing strategy. It should feature on your letterheads, website, business cards, e-shots, invoices - in fact on almost everything you send out or use for marketing yourself.

- **Your logo's purpose**

  Your logo is intended to be the "face" of your company: it is a graphical display of your company's unique identity, and by appropriately using colours, fonts and images it enables clients to quickly identify and understand what your company is about and what it stands for. It should also be consistent with the fonts, colours and design choices across all your business and marketing materials.

- **The design**

  A good logo should be unique and clear. It should be designed in a way that provides some sense of meaning about you and what your company offers.

- **Brand Identity**

  Your logo needs to look professional. It should blend with the fonts and designs used on your website and other branding. There's nothing worse than a good, professionally designed logo, which then stands out like a sore thumb among a jumble of mixed colours and fonts. Keep your branding consistent and 'clean'.

- **Return on investment**

  As clients grow to know, like and trust your brand they are more likely to respond positively by choosing to work with you rather than poorly branded competitors.

Images

The images you use in your marketing and branding will play a big part in

- Building your name, reputation and brand

- Social media - it's all about good content and images

- Your website – great, professional photos really do make all the difference

You can get very good free or reasonably priced images from sites such as Pixaby and Fotolia (now Adobe Stock).
https://pixabay.com/
https://en.fotolia.com

Never use photos or images that have copyright attached to them unless you are prepared to pay for them.

PRACTICAL TASK #15

Take a look at one of the most commonly used sites for logos: LogoNerds. They provide a good but cheaper logo design option. Normally I would suggest paying a little bit more for a graphic designer who can create you a unique logo, as this can help you to stand out from the crowd, but LogoNerds are a great starting point for new businesses.
http://www.logonerds.com/

You can also post on Facebook group and ask if there are any members who could design one for you.

Business Cards

Your business card is your calling card and reminds people of who you are and how they can contact you. They are essential to any business. Your card should be of a good - but not necessarily expensive – quality and unique to you, that is to say it should contain:

- Your logo
- Your telephone and mobile numbers
- Your website address
- Your social media profile handles
- Your professional email address
- Your name
- Your company name (if this is not stated on your logo)

- Remember that your business card has two sides, so use them both (it is a little bit more expensive, but well worth it!). On the reverse of your card list 5 of your services/benefits to the client, for example, 'Professional Admin and Business Support Services' or 'Registered with the ICO for the purposes of GDPR'. Remember a contact you meet at a networking event may want to write on the back of it and so bear this in mind when designing your card – if it is 'glossy' it may be difficult to write on!

- QR Code (more on this shortly)

- Include a call to action too should you have room, for example "Want to know more? Call (telephone number) now for a free consultation".

Be consistent: as with your logo, stick to the same colours and fonts throughout your branding and marketing, be clear about who you are and what you are about.

QR Code (Quick Response Code)

A QR code is a great way of enabling people to access your website using their smartphones. They scan the code, which will take them directly to your website or anything else that contains a URL of your choosing. They're free and a great marketing tool. I use my QR codes on e-shots and business cards. The QR Code generator I use is at:
http://www.qrstuff.com/

PRACTICAL TASK #16

Go to the QR Stuff website and create your own code. If you don't have a website yet, then just use a URL from any reputable website for practice purposes. This is so you can see how it all works and how to create a QR code for yourself. You can delete it afterwards. Here's how you do it:

- Go to **http://www.qrstuff.com/**

- 1. Data Type – website URL should be selected (this is usually already done)

- 2. Content – copy and paste your website URL (the web address) into this box

- 3. Foreground Colour – leave this as it is. You can change the colour but you have to pay for this and it's not really necessary for your purposes

- 4. QR Code Preview – click on 'Download QR Code'. This may open up a new window and so look for this flashing at the bottom of your screen.

Well done! You've now created your first QR Code. Save this on your PC/laptop in a marketing folder. Remember when saving your QR Code to add a title that refers to what it relates to e.g QRC-landing page – QRC-blog page. This will help you locate the correct code when you are ready to add it to your marketing material. You may create several QR Codes over time and this is why it is best to get into the habit of naming each one as you create it.

You can test that it works by downloading an app on your smartphone and scanning the code you have just created. You can then watch how it takes you to the relevant page on your website. The apps I use are 'QR Reader' and 'Quick Scan' for iPhone.

When marketing try to remember the concept of the 'six degrees of separation'. This is the theory that everyone and everything is six or fewer contacts away, by way of introduction, from any other person. It takes time to make connections, but with considered, consistent marketing you'll get there!

Getting your first client

When you have your first client – **go out and celebrate**! Treat yourself to something nice: a few drinks with friends, a meal out with family, whatever you feel you would like to do to share your success story – you deserve it!

I found my clients through on-line networking, my website face to face networking, 'word of mouth' (referrals) and by asking current clients if they knew anyone among their own contacts who may benefit from my services. You never really know where your clients will come from, but the more structured your marketing methods are, the greater your reach and potential for success will be.

PART 4 – HELP AND RESOURCES

I love helping people and I guess that is one of the reasons I do the job I do. Never feel too embarrassed or ashamed to ask for help; we all need help in our lives and no one knows absolutely everything. I believe that the ones who ask for help are the ones who progress faster and better when starting out on their own. Trying to wear too many hats can often distract you from the bigger picture. Help is always available - you just need to look or ask for it. The content of this book will help you to start and develop your own virtual assistant business.

Working from home is not just about equipment, it's about knowledge too. I've listed below some of my favourite apps, plug-ins and programmes and I recommend you explore these carefully, familiarise yourself with what they do and what comes for free and what you have to pay for.

You will find many of these programmes invaluable. They will help you (and your client too!) to work more effectively and efficiently. Some of these links can also be found in the body of this book, but I have listed them again below for your convenience. The more you know, the more of an asset you become to your clients!

Apps, plug-ins, programmes, business loans, info

- **Word, Excel. PowerPoint, Outlook, SharePoint**, these come as part of the Office 365 programme – you also get a business email address with this package **https://products.office.com/en-gb/compare-all-microsoft-office-products?tab=1**

- **Google Docs, Sheets, Forms and Slides https://www.google.co.uk/docs/about/**

- **Google Calendar** - a great way to share your diary, its it free to use and can be used on most mobile devices. You will need to create Google account if you do not have one
https://www.google.com/calendar/about/

- **Calendly** – great tool for diarising and scheduling meetings
https://calendly.com/

- **Doodle Poll** – another great tool for scheduling meetings and finding out who is available for dates
https://doodle.com/en_GB/

- **E-shots/Newsletters** – these programmes let you create professional looking e-shots/newsletters
https://madmimi.com
https://mailchimp.com

- **Webinar programmes** – these programmes help you to prepare and deliver on-line webinars. You may wish to give small free webinars to showcase your knowledge and skills and to help raise your profile. Although you will not need this to begin with, you may find it very useful at a later date for your own purposes or perhaps to help a client. A popular programme to try is GotoWebinar
http://www.gotomeeting.com/webinar

- **Dropbox** – cloud based document storage and share. Many of your client will use this, it's a great way to share files and collaborate with your clients and associate VAs
https://www.dropbox.com

- **Microsoft One Drive** – cloud based document storage
https://onedrive.live.com/about/en-gb/plans/

- **Teamwork** - Project Manager
  https://www.teamwork.com

- **Capsule CRM** – customer relationship management (CRM) software
  https://capsulecrm.com/

- **ZoHo** – CRM system **https://www.zoho.eu**

- **Eventbrite** – great for finding local networking events etc in your area while also sharing events you might like to organise yourself as you progress
  https://www.eventbrite.co.uk/

- **Survey Monkey** – great for creating surveys
  https://www.surveymonkey.com

- **Evernote** - I only use the free basic system but it works fine for me. Capture, organise and share notes
  https://evernote.com/

- **Cam Scanner** – great little app that allows you to scan documents and turn them into PDFs that you can send from your phone
  https://www.camscanner.com/

- **We Transfer** – this is a great way to send to large files to your clients. It is free to use. I use this to send files that are too big to attach to an email, or if I want to ensure the file is sent securely
  https://wetransfer.com/

- **E-signature Tools** – these are great tools for getting documents signed electronically easily and quickly without the need for a scanner. Some are free and some are paid for – which you choose will depend on

how you are going to use it and for how long. I personally only ever use the free versions as I do not use them to create documents, only to send them to a client or associate for signature.
https://www.hellosign.com/
https://go.docusign.com
https://www.signable.co.uk

- **Hootsuite** – this is a free social medial management tool that allows you to create and schedule blog posts across a variety of social media platforms
https://hootsuite.com

- **Invoicely** – this is a very simple and easy to use programme for creating invoices. There is a free version but it has their branding on it, or you can pay to have your own branding
https://invoicely.com/

- **SendOwl** – a great way to sell digital products
https://www.sendowl.com

- **Time Tracker Tools** – these are a good way of keeping track of the time you are working for each of your clients
https://minutedock.com/
https://myhours.com/
https://toggl.com/

- **Spreadsheet Tips** – need help with Excel – this is a great place to get tips
http://spreadsheetpage.com/index.php/tips

- **Transcription Programmes**
http://www.winscribe.co.uk/

http://www.expressscribe.co.uk/

- **https://smallpdf.com/** - great for joining a few PDF files together.

- **https://tinytake.com/** - for recording a video of on screen steps – you get about 5 mins recording time for free. Great for 'how to' videos

- **https://www.receipt-bank.com/** - great for handling receipts

- **Start Ups** – news, loans, events, information and help
  https://www.virginstartup.org/news
  https://www.virginstartup.org/start-up-loans
  http://www.fsb.org.uk/
  https://www.princes-trust.org.uk
  http://www.britishchambers.org.uk/
  https://www.gov.uk/business-support-helpline

FREE templates

If you would like a free copy of any of the templates below, drop me a line at erica@wrightbusinesssupportcentre.co.uk with proof of purchase of this book and I will be happy to email them to you (please let me know which ones you would like – thank you):
- Business Plan
- Invoice
- First and second reminder letters
- Client and equipment checklists
- Client welcome letter
- Client Assessment Form
- Client Proposal

PART 5 - THE LEGAL STUFF

There are a few things you will need to do when setting yourself up as self-employed.

Registering with HMRC

Register with HMRC. This web address will take you to the information and registration details you'll need.
https://www.gov.uk/working-for-yourself/what-you-need-to-do

Paying National Insurance

Arrange to pay National Insurance contributions
More information on N.I. can be found here:
https://www.gov.uk/self-employed-national-insurance-rates

Sole Trader or Limited Company?

Decide whether to set up as self-employed, sole trader or a limited company. There are 'for' and 'against' for each of these and when making the decision, I would always recommend you speak to a qualified accountant if you are unsure. Most accountants will give you free advice on this matter.

Sole traders run their own business and are responsible for that business as an individual. However, you can employ people. Being a sole trader means you are responsible for the business, not that you have to work on your own.

With a limited company the liability of members of the company is limited to what they have invested or guaranteed.

164

It is a little too complicated to go into great detail in this guide but you can find more information and what this entails here: **https://www.gov.uk/limited-company-formation/register-your-company**

PRACTICAL TASK #17

Call HMRC. I found them to be very helpful when I first started out. Explain what you are planning to do and ask for help and advice on how to register to pay National Insurance, what you will need to pay and how, if after exploring the above link, you are still unsure.

You have now set up your own business and your journey has begun!

Celebrate your success and carry on the good work. I wish you all the best for the future.

Running your own business is a journey and not a destination. You never really know where it can take you, so enjoy the adventure.

I hope this book makes your journey far easier than it was for me when I first started out.

Good Luck!

ABOUT ERICA

Having spent over 20 years in various roles within the legal industry (yes - a long time!) working in London and Manchester, I grew tired of working within that specific sector and set about looking for a new, fresh challenge. It was important to me to (1) offer a personal and bespoke service to very high standards (2) find something that would give me the end of day job satisfaction I was looking for and (3) help other people by using the vast business support and administration knowledge I had stuffed into my brain. After long and careful consideration, it became apparent to me that the only way I was going to be able to fulfil my ambitions was to set up my own company.

But this posed me three questions:

(1) What did I want to do?

(2) What need was I going to fill and how?

(3) Whose needs would I be filling?

The answer to the first question was easy – administration and business support. Why? Because I was very passionate about these two specific aspects of my career, it was what I enjoyed doing most and it was where all my knowledge, skills and experience had sprung from.

The second question was thought provoking and I felt the best way to answer this was to get it straight from the 'horse's mouth' so to speak. I set about speaking with business owners and charitable organisations about what *they* thought would help *them* to grow and develop.

The answer to the third question came from a mixture of what I personally wanted – job satisfaction, new challenges and to help other people – and from the answers given by business owners and charitable organisations in response to question 2.

After gathering all the information I needed, **Wright Business Support Centre** was born, offering a personal, bespoke and flexible business outsourcing solution based on filling the needs of micro to small businesses and charitable organisations.

The greatest challenge I faced when I first started my new business was getting the message across to other businesses and organisations about what I did, as many just didn't get it. They didn't fully appreciate that I offered so much more than just admin support, and that the business outsourcing solutions I could offer were far more outreaching than they could imagine. I created my new website to try to answer as many of the more frequently asked questions as I possibly could, and I began networking and building professional relationships with business owners and charitable organisations. I posted regularly on social media and nowadays a large part of my work comes via recommendation and my website.

I don't want to make any bones about it: to run a business and be self-employed **is hard work** and so be under no illusions as to what's required. You need dedication, determination and a will to succeed. I did it - and have not looked back. I cannot imagine myself *ever* wanting to go back to being employed. I love being my own boss, deciding on the course of my business and choosing my own clients. Yes, its hard work, but worth every bit of effort. The personal satisfaction you feel with success is unbeatable.

It took me over two years to build my business foundations from scratch. Earning my reputation within the business market place, building my brand, making contacts, learning how to run my own business and building my client base: it was a massive learning curve – but one I embraced with enthusiasm and excitement – with a few nervous moments thrown in!

The contacts I made - clients as well as associates - played a significant part in my business growth, development and success.

I am often approached by fellow virtual assistants who are in difficulty and need help. These requests arrive in all forms - in person, via telephone, personal messages through social media and through my website. That's why I decided to write this book. It provides answers to the most common questions I am asked.

Having been in the legal, admin and business support industry for nearly 30 years, supporting all forms of business and organisation, it is not possible for me to put every little thing I know into this book. It would quickly become a huge encyclopaedia! I hope all of the knowledge and experience I have poured into this book is useful and helps you on your own journey.

NOTES

NOTES

Printed in Poland
by Amazon Fulfillment
Poland Sp. z o.o., Wrocław

40634843R00101